The Natural Woman's Guide to Hormone Replacement Therapy

An Alternative Approach

M. Sara Rosenthal, Ph. D.

New Page Books
A Division of The Career Press, Inc.
Franklin Lakes, NJ

THE NATURAL WOMAN'S GUIDE TO HORMONE REPLACEMENT THERAPY
EDITED BY KATE HENCHES
TYPESET BY EILEEN DOW MUNSON
Cover design by Foster & Foster, Inc.
Printed in the U.S.A. by Book-mart Press

To order this title, please call toll-free 1-800-CAREER-1 (NJ and Canada: 201-848-0310) to order using VISA or MasterCard, or for further information on books from Career Press.

The Career Press, Inc., 3 Tice Road, PO Box 687,
Franklin Lakes, NJ 07417
www.careerpress.com
www.newpagebooks.com

Library of Congress Cataloging-in-Publication Data

Rosenthal, M. Sara.
    The natural woman's guide to hormone replacement therapy : an alternative approach / by M. Sara Rosenthal.
        p. cm.
    Includes bibliographical references and index.
    ISBN 1-56414-681-2 (pbk.)
        1. Menopause—Complications—Alternative treatment. 2. Menopause—Hormone therapy. 3. Naturopathy. I. Title.

RG186.R66 2003
618.1'75061—dc21

2003050981

Disclaimer

The purpose of this book is to educate. It is sold with the understanding that the author and publisher shall have neither liability nor responsibility for any injury caused or alleged to be caused directly or indirectly by the information contained in this book. Although every effort has been made to ensure its accuracy, the book's contents should not be construed as medical advice. Each person's health needs are unique. To obtain recommendations appropriate to your particular situation, please consult a qualified healthcare provider. The herbal information in this book is provided for education purposes only and is not meant to be used without consulting a qualified health practitioner who is trained in herbal medicine.

Acknowledgments

I wish to thank the following people, whose expertise and dedication helped to lay so much of the groundwork for this book (listed alphabetically): Gillian Arsenault, M.D., C.C.F.P., IB.L.C., F.R.C.P.; Pamela Craig, M.D., F.A.C.S., Ph.D.; Masood Kahthamee, M.D., F.A.C.O.G.; Debra Lander, M.D., F.R.C.P.; Gary May, M.D., F.R.C.P.; James McSherry, M.B., Ch.B., F.C.F.P., FR.C.G.P., F.A.A.F.P., F.A.B.M.P.; Suzanne Pratt, M.D., FA.C.OG.; Wm. Warren Rudd, M.D., F.R.C.S., F.A.C.S., colon and rectal surgeon and founder and director of The Rudd Clinic For Diseases of the Colon and Rectum (Toronto); and Robert Volpe, M.D., F.R.C.P., F.A.C.P.

I'd also like to extend my sincere gratitude to William Harvey, Ph.D., L.L.B., former director, University of Toronto Joint Centre for Bioethics, whose devotion to bioethics has inspired me, continues to support my work, and makes it possible for me to have the courage to question and challenge issues in health care and medical ethics; Irving Rootman, Ph.D., former director, University of Toronto Centre for Health Promotion, who continues to encourage my interest in primary prevention and health promotion issues; and Helen Lenskyj, Ph.D., professor, Department of Sociology and Equity Studies, Ontario Institute for Studies in Education/University of Toronto, and Laura M. Purdy, Ph.D., Philosopher and Bioethist, Wells College, Ithaca, who have been central figures in my understanding the complexities of women's health issues and feminist bioethics.

Contents

Introduction:
What to Do About Hormone Replacement Therapy

In July 2001, a study by the U.S. National Heart, Lung and Blood Institute, part of a huge research program called the Women's Health Initiative (WHI), suggested that Hormone Replacement Therapy (HRT) should not be recommended for long-term use. In fact, the results were so alarming, the study was halted before its completion date. It was found that Prempro, a combination of estrogen and progestin, which was a "standard issue" HRT formulation for post-menopausal women, increased the risk of invasive breast cancer, heart disease, stroke, and pulmonary embolisms (blood clots). However, Prempro *did* reduce the incidence of bone fractures from osteoporosis and colon cancer. Nevertheless, the idea that HRT is a long-term "fountain of youth" is slowly dissolving. The study participants were informed in a letter that they should stop taking their pills. HRT, used in the short-term to relieve menopausal symptoms, is still considered a good option, and there was no evidence to suggest that short-term use of HRT was harmful. The study only has implications for women on HRT for long-term use—something that was recommended to millions of women during the past 20 years because of perceived protection against heart disease.

In 1998, an earlier trial, known as the Heart and Estrogen/ Progesin Replacement Study (HERS), looked at whether HRT was reduced in women who already had heart disease. HRT was not found to have any beneficial effect. Women who were at risk for breast cancer were never advised to go on HRT; similarly, women who had suffered a stroke or considered at risk for blood clots were also never considered good candidates for HRT. It had long been known that breast cancer was a risk of long-term HRT, as well as stroke and blood clots. However, many women made the HRT decision based on the fact that it was long believed to protect women from heart disease. Millions of women are now questioning whether they should be on HRT in light of these facts and findings.

Today, the only thing the "experts" can agree on is that the HRT decision is highly individual and must be an informed decision, where all of the possible risks and benefits of taking—or not taking—HRT are disclosed. Women with a family history of breast cancer were never considered good HRT candidates. So, for this group of women, things have not changed. However, women who were considered at higher risk for heart disease due to family history or other risk factors, such as Type 2 diabetes, are now more confused than ever.

As a bioethicist and sociologist who specializes in women's health, and as the author of numerous books on women's health, I am alarmed, but not surprised, by the findings of the HRT studyies. I have been questioning the medicalization and pathologizing of menopause for years, along with millions of women who have taken their health into their own hands, turning to natural forms of hormone replacement therapy through phytoestrogens (plant estrogens), natural hormone therapy (NRT), or natural progesterone therapy. For too long, women have been disempowered by a male-constructed medical system in which women's bodies have become fodder for experimental medicine without their genuine informed consent. But many women have discovered, through diet, movement, herbal alternatives, and natural forms of progesterone and estrogen, that they can take charge of their health once more.

The lessons learned from this HRT study are not new; we have lived through this story before. Diethylstilbestrol (DES), the Dalkon Shield, and Phen/Fen are all examples from the same women's health narrative.

I frequently get questions at my Website (*www.sarahealth.com*) from browsers and readers who are worried about the "new facts of menopause." The answer I always give is this: the road to good health is paved through self-education. This book is designed to help you educate yourself about your health options during perimenopause and postmenopause.

Life After Periods

Considering how many women are just beginning to *really* live at 50, it seems absurd to read about menopause, doesn't it? How could *you* possibly relate to books about "enjoying your grandchildren" or "preparing for midlife" or "golden years" or the dozens of other euphemisms for "hey—you're getting old!" Many of you probably have young children at home—or young lovers. Many of you are in the peak of your careers. Many of you are just re-singled, coming out of long-term marriages or relationships. Somebody tell them to turn back the clock! You're just gettin' rollin'!

In 2001, almost 20 million women in the United States were recorded as being between ages 45 and 54—the largest number of women in that age group in all of history. This generation is already de-medicalizing and demystifying menopause, repositioning it not as a disease, but as a natural stage in life. It is up to you to take back your body and make your own choices about how you want to live and the quality of life you want to maintain or enjoy. Native American folklore records that we are in the midst of massive Earth changes that will climax around 2013. It's been said that these Earth changes will bring heat, floods, and incredible upheaval to the world's population. By then, more than 50 million women will have achieved menopause and will have gone through their own heat (via hot flashes), floods (via heavy bleeding) and upheaval. Some question whether we are entering a "mass menopause" or "collective menopause." "Earth changes" notwithstanding, the "mass menopause" that will take place in the next few years will be felt. Your menopause, in many ways, is a social menopause—a time for our culture to *stop* and *change* the way we think about aging.

This chapter gives you the facts about *perimenopause* (a term that literally means "around menopause"—the time where the physical signs and changes of menopause make their appearance), and both the short- and long-term consequences of estrogen loss. "What To Eat" (pages 38 through 43) provides you with an extensive body of information about herbal remedies, therapies, and alternatives to pharmaceutical drugs typically prescribed to women approaching menopause. And "How To Move" (pages 44 through 45) offers a range of activities, postures, and exercises that can help to offset the general discomforts of perimenopause and estrogen loss.

How Menopause Became a Disease

If menopause is a natural stage in your life, why is it treated by the medical profession as a "disease"? Why are words like *symptoms* used to describe the natural changes associated with estrogen loss? Why are you led to believe that you now have a "hormone deficiency syndrome" resulting from estrogen loss, and treated as though you are in a "diseased state" when you are perfectly well? The answer is simple: You live in a Western culture in which *everything* is medicalized and pathologized— from womb to tomb. It's not just menopause that is being medicalized. This trend can be seen with pregnancy and prenatal care, pediatric care (for example, millions of children are being diagnosed with behavior disorders that in the past were considered normal), mental health (where people are put on medication for social causes of angst, anxiety, and depression), and so on. In short, *all* the normal physical processes of the human body have been "pathologized" by medicine. But more frequently, it is women's normal physical processes, which are subject to the mass marketing of prevention drugs or not-well-tested therapies. In our 20s and 30s, we are sold drugs to prevent pregnancy and "regulate" our cycles. In our 30s and 40s (and now 50s), we are put on fertility drugs to "regulate" our cycles so we *can* get pregnant. And in our 50s and beyond, we are put on estrogen replacement drugs to "regulate" our cycles, too, and to prevent health problems associated with estrogen loss. There are lots other health conditions that sell questionable drugs to women, but to date the number one best-seller for pharmaceutical companies is hormone replacement therapy. And with the "mass menopause" beginning, you don't have to be a stock broker to guess that HRT "stock" stands to triple.

The Lost Hormone

It wasn't until the 1960s that the idea of giving estrogen to menopausal women took hold (which coincided with the introduction of the pill). A 1963 article by Dr. Robert Wilson entitled "The Fate of the Nontreated Menopausal Woman: A Plea for the Maintenance of Adequate Estrogen from Puberty to the Grave," in the *Journal of the American Geriatrics Society* was the breakthrough article that promoted HRT. This article outlined the "serious consequences" of estrogen loss: heart disease, hypertension, osteoporosis, "tough, dry, scaly and inelastic skin, flabby atrophic breasts, and shrinking labia." The final blow came when Wilson stated that menopause was a "mutilation of the whole body [and that] no woman can be sure of escaping the horror of this living decay." Thus, a new disease was coined, and the menopause "industry" was born. To Wilson, estrogen loss was just like any other hormone deficiency, such as insulin in diabetes. If the lost hormone could be replaced, it *should* be replaced. This is the attitude that has prevailed.

Since Wilson, menopause "apologists" have surfaced in abundance; these are researchers who explain menopause as an accident of nature. The "apology" is an apology to women for nature's failings. You see, a woman's ovaries were supposed to work until she died, but because of a huge increase in human longevity within a short time span, there is now a gap in the natural life of a woman and the natural life of her ovaries. The message of this apology is: "It's all a big mistake; you weren't supposed to live to see menopause. It's not your fault; medicine can fix this." (In recent years the phenomenon of "andropause"—a deficiency of testosterone—is being sold to men as the answer to their fatigue and loss of "pep" in their midlife.)

Natural Menopause vs. "Discomfort Control"

Today, there are more than 20 million U.S. women over 50. It seems absurd to suggest that this enormous number of women are all "sick" and need to take medication. Yet, this is the reality of our times. In essence, we are medicating huge numbers of well, healthy women with powerful drugs. Should doctors be doing this? Or, should doctors sit back and allow unnecessary discomfort and suffering when that suffering can be prevented?

Only *you* have the answer. If you feel physical discomfort and want your discomfort to be treated, you have that right. If you want to do everything you can to prevent long-term complications of estrogen loss (such as osteoporosis), you have that right, also. And you have the right *not* be judged by your peers for choosing to be relieved of your discomfort, or choosing preventative therapies for serious diseases associated with estrogen loss. Would your grandmother have chosen estrogen if it were offered to her? Would your grandmother have chosen to be uncomfortable when comfort was an option? Would your grandmother have chosen to experience a hip fracture or opt for information on preventing such a fate?

On the other hand, if you want to embrace the changes of your body as something nature intended and experience your menopause as a "rite of passage," so to speak, you ought not be coerced into viewing these natural changes as a "disease" or coerced into "treating" the natural rhythms and flows of your body. In many non-Western cultures, menopause is considered a powerful time for women, where they are perceived as vessels for powerful energies that flow through them. Why should you be forced to deny yourself this powerful experience? You have the right **not** to be judged by your doctors or peers for choosing "natural menopause" (just as you would not be judged for choosing natural childbirth).

Many of you will fall between these two viewpoints. You may decide to investigate diet, herbs, and simple lifestyle changes to offset your discomforts. Within this chapter are a number of solutions for you to choose. Mix 'n match; there are no rules.

Natural Menopause

Your first period (menarche) and your last (menopause) have much in common. They are both *gradual* processes that women ease into. A woman doesn't suddenly wake up to find herself in menopause any more than a young girl wakes up to find herself in puberty. However, when menopause occurs *surgically*—the by-product of an oophorectomy, ovarian failure following a hysterectomy, or certain cancer therapies—it can be an extremely jarring process. *One out of every three women in North America will not make it to the age of 60 with her uterus intact.* These women may indeed wake up one morning to find themselves in menopause, and, as a result, will suffer far more noticeable and severe signs of menopause than their natural menopause counterparts. It is because of *surgical* menopause that *Hormonal Replacement Therapy* (HRT) and *Estrogen Replacement Therapy* (ERT or "unopposed estrogen") have become such hotly debated issues in women's health. The loss of estrogen, in particular, leads to drastic changes in the body's chemistry that trigger a more aggressive aging process. Menopause is a recent phenomenon in our society. Anywhere from 60 to 100 years ago, women simply died prior to menopause. Only in this century have women ever outlived their ovaries.

The word *menstrual* comes from the Latin word *mens*, meaning "month;" but the root word of month is "moon." The menstrual cycle actually follows the lunar calendar, not the English calendar, and in Greek, menstruation actually means "moon change." *Menopause* is a Greek term taken from the words *menos*, which means "month," and *pause*, which means "arrest"—the arrest of the menstrual cycle. In many native cultures, menopause can be tracked by the moon. The last period, it is said, falls on the 14th full moon after the onset of the signs of menopause. And if you track back 13 full moons on a sheet of paper after your periods have stopped, this tracking system is apparently pretty accurate. Apparently, by sleeping where the full moon can shine on your face when you're in the throes of menopausal changes, or by sleeping in a dark room during the full moon, and simulating moonlight with a light, your physical changes will be eased.

When menopause occurs naturally, it tends to take place anywhere between the ages of 48 and 52, but it can occur as early as your late 30s, or as late as your mid-50s. When menopause occurs *before* 45, it is technically considered "early menopause" but, just as menarche is genetically predetermined, so is menopause. For an average woman with an unremarkable medical history, what she eats or does in terms of activity will *not* influence the timing of her menopause. However, women who have had chemotherapy or have been exposed to high levels of radiation (such as radiation therapy in their pelvic area for cancer treatment) may go into earlier menopause. In any event, the average age of menopause is 50–51.

Other causes that have been cited to trigger an early menopause include mumps. In small groups of women, the infection causing the mumps has been known to spread to the ovaries, prematurely shutting them down. Some women with specific autoimmune diseases, such as lupus or rheumatoid arthritis, develop antibodies (to their own ovaries) that attack the ovaries.

The Stages of Natural Menopause

Socially, the word *menopause* refers to a process, not a precise moment in the life of your menstrual cycle. But medically, the word *menopause* does *indeed* refer to one precise moment: the date of your last period. However, the events preceding and following menopause amount to a huge change for women both physically and socially.

Physically, this process is divided into four stages:

1. **Premenopause:** Although some doctors may refer to a 32-old woman in her childbearing years as "premenopausal," this is not really an appropriate label. The term *premenopause* ideally refers to women on the "cusp" of menopause. Their periods have just *started* to get irregular, but they do not yet experience any classic signs of menopause, such as hot flashes or vaginal dryness. Woman in premenopause are usually in their mid- to late 40s. If your doctor tells you that you're premenopausal, you might want to ask him or her how he or she is using the term.

2. **Perimenopause:** This term refers to women who are in the thick of menopause; their cycles are wildly erratic and they are experiencing hot flashes and vaginal dryness. This label is applicable for about four years, including the first two years prior to the official "last" period to the next two years following the last menstrual period. Women who are perimenopausal will be in the age groups previously discussed, averaging to about age 51.

3. **Menopause:** This term refers to your final menstrual period. You will not be able to pinpoint your final period until you've been completely free from periods for one year. Then, you count back to the last period you charted, and *that date* is the *date of your menopause. Important: After more than one year of no menstrual periods, any vaginal bleeding is now considered abnormal.*

4. **Postmenopause:** This term refers to the last third of most women's lives, ranging from women who have been free of menstrual periods for at least four years to women celebrating their 100th birthdays. In other words, once you're past menopause, you'll be referred to as postmenopausal for the rest of your life. Sometimes, the terms postmenopausal and perimenopausal are used interchangeably, but this is technically inaccurate.

In a *social* context, however, nobody really bothers to break down menopause this precisely. When you see the phrase "menopausal" in a magazine article, you are seeing what's become acceptable medical slang, referring to women who are premenopausal and perimenopausal—a time frame that *includes* the actual menopause. When you see the word *postmenopausal* in a magazine article, you are seeing another accepted medical slang, which includes women who are in perimenopause and "official" postmenopause.

Determining premenopause or perimenopause

When you begin to notice the signs of menopause, discussed next, either you'll suspect the approach of menopause on your own, or your doctor will put two and two together when you report your "bizarre symptoms." There are two very simple tests that will accurately determine what's going on and what stage of menopause you're in. Your FSH levels will dramatically rise as your ovaries begin to shut down; these levels are easily checked from one blood test. In addition, your vaginal walls will thin, and the cells lining the vagina will not contain as much estrogen. Your doctor will simply do a Pap-like smear on your vaginal walls—simple and painless—and then just analyze the smear to check for vaginal "atrophy," the thinning and drying out of your vagina. In addition, as I'll discuss shortly, you need to keep track of your periods and chart them as they become irregular. Your menstrual pattern will be an additional clue to your doctor about whether your pre or perimenopausal.

Signs of Natural Menopause

In the past, a long list of hysterical symptoms have been attributed to the "change of life," but medically there are really just three classic *short-term* signs of menopause: erratic periods, hot flashes, and vaginal dryness. All three of these signs are caused by a decrease in estrogen. As for the emotional signs of menopause, such as irritability, mood swings, melancholy, and so on, they are actually caused by a *rise in follicle stimulating hormone (FSH)*. As the cycle changes and the ovaries' egg supplies dwindle, FSH is secreted in very high amounts and reach a lifetime peak—as much as 15 times higher; it's the body's way of trying to "jump-start" the ovarian engine. This is *why* the urine of menopausal women is used to produce Human Menopausal Gonadotropin (HMG), the potent fertility drug that consists of pure FSH.

Every woman entering menopause will experience a change in her menstrual cycle. However, not all women will experience hot flashes or even notice vaginal changes. This is particularly true if a woman is overweight. Estrogen is stored in fat cells, which is why overweight women also tend to be more at risk for estrogen-dependent cancers. What happens is that the fat cells convert fat into estrogen, creating a type of estrogen reserve that the body will use during menopause, which can reduce the severity of estrogen loss. This can actually be considered a positive side effect to being overweight.

Erratic periods

Every woman will begin to experience an irregular cycle before her last period. Cycles may become longer or shorter with long bouts of amennorhea. There will also be flow changes, where periods may suddenly become light and scanty, or very heavy and crampy. The heavy bleeding occurs because of a sudden drop in progesterone levels (this is why *all* women get their periods). But when progesterone levels are higher than normal for a premenopausal women, the uterine lining just keeps growing thicker. Then, when you do bleed, it just floods and gushes (and clots...oh boy!). It's not unusual to bleed heavily for as long as 10–14 days. You will lose iron when you bleed this heavily. See the What to Eat section for iron-rich herbs and foods (pages 38–43).

Keeping your cool about hot flashes

Roughly 85 percent of all pre- and perimenopausal women experience what are known as "hot flashes." Eastern cultures view a hot flash as a release of "cosmic electricity" (known as kundalini energies), which not only "rewires" your individual nervous system, but gives you "healing energies" for your entire community. The intensity of a hot flash can be compared to the intensity felt during anger, orgasm, or even enlightenment, which all involve "kundalini energies," too.

Hot flashes can begin when periods are either still regular or have just started to become irregular. The hot flashes usually stop one to two years after your final menstrual period. A hot flash can feel different for each woman. Some women experience a feeling of warmth in their face and upper body; some women experience hot flashes as a simultaneous sweating with chills. Some women feel anxious, tense, dizzy, or nauseated just before the hot flash; some feel tingling in their fingers or heart palpitations just prior. Some women will experience their hot flashes during the day; others will experience them at night and may wake up so wet from perspiration that they need to change their bed sheets and/or nightclothes.

Nobody really understands what causes hot flashes, but researchers believe that it has to do with mixed signals from the hypothalamus, which controls both body temperature and sex hormones. Normally, when the body is too warm, the hypothalamus sends a chemical message to the heart to cool off the body by pumping more blood, causing the blood vessels under the skin to dilate, which makes you perspire. During menopause, however, it's believed that the hypothalamus gets confused and sends this "cooling off" signal at the wrong times. A hot flash is not the same as being overheated. Although the skin temperature often rises between 4 and 8 degrees Fahrenheit, the internal body temperature drops, creating this odd sensation. Why does the hypothalamus get so confused? Decreasing levels of estrogen. We know this because when synthetic estrogen is given to replace natural estrogen in the body, hot flashes disappear. Some researchers believe that a decrease in leutinizing hormone (LH) is also a key factor, and a variety of other hormones that influence body temperature are being looked at as well. Although hot flashes are harmless in terms of health risks, they are disquieting and stressful. Certain groups of women will experience more severe hot flashes than others:

> **Women who are in surgical menopause** (page 28).

> **Women who are thin.** When there's less fat on the body to store estrogen reserves, physical changes associated with estrogen loss are more severe.

> **Women who don't sweat easily.** An ability to sweat makes extreme temperatures easier to tolerate. Women who have trouble sweating may experience more severe flashes.

Just as you must chart your periods when your cycles become irregular, it's also important to chart your hot flashes. Keep track of when the flashes occur, how long they last, and their intensity number (pick a number from one to 10). This will help you determine a pattern for the flashes and allow you to prepare for them in advance—which will reduce the stress involved in the flashes to begin with. It's also crucial to report your hot flashes to your doctor—just as you would any changes in your cycle. Hot flashes can also indicate other health problems, such as circulatory problems, and so on.

What can I do about my hot flashes?

Short of taking ERT or HRT, the only thing you can do about your hot flashes is to lessen your discomfort by adjusting your lifestyle to cope with the flashes. The more comfortable you are, the less intense your flashes will feel. Once you establish a pattern by charting the flashes, you can do a few things around the time of day your flashes occur. Some suggestions:

➤ Avoid synthetic clothing, such as polyester, because it traps perspiration.

➤ Use only 100 percent cotton bedding if you have night sweats.

➤ Avoid clothing with high necks and long sleeves.

➤ Dress in layers.

➤ Keep cold drinks handy.

➤ If you smoke, cut down or quit. Smoking constricts blood vessels and can intensify and prolong a flash.

➤ Avoid "trigger" foods such as caffeine, alcohol, spicy foods, sugars, and large meals. Substitute herbal teas for coffee or regular tea.

➤ Discuss the benefits of taking vitamin E supplements with your doctor. Evidence suggests that it's essential for proper circulation and the production of sex hormones.

➤ Exercise to improve your circulation.

➤ Reduce your exposure to the sun; sunburn will aggravate your hot flashes because burned skin cannot regulate heat as effectively. (The sun is discussed further on page 30 [skin changes].)

Vaginal changes

Estrogen loss will also cause vaginal changes. Because it is the production of estrogen that causes the vagina to continuously stay moist and elastic through its natural secretions, the loss of estrogen will cause the vagina to become drier, thinner, and less elastic. This may also cause the vagina to shrink slightly in terms of width and length. In addition, the reduction in vaginal secretions causes the vagina to be less acidic. This can put you at risk for more vaginal infections. As a result of these vaginal changes, you'll notice a change in your sexual activity. Your vagina may take longer to become lubricated, or you may have to depend on lubricants to have comfortable intercourse.

Estrogen loss can affect other parts of your sex life as well. Your sexual libido may actually increase because testosterone levels can rise when estrogen levels drop. (The general rule is that your levels of testosterone will either stay the same or increase.) However, women who *do* experience an increase in sexual desire will also be frustrated that their vaginas are not accommodating their needs. First, there is the lubrication problem: More stimulation is required to lubricate the vagina naturally. Second, a decrease in estrogen means that less blood flows to the vagina and clitoris, which means that orgasm may be more difficult to achieve or may not last as long as it normally has in the past. Other changes involve the breasts. Normally, estrogen causes blood to flow into the breasts during arousal, which makes the nipples more erect, sensitive, and responsive. Estrogen loss causes less blood to flow to the breasts, which makes them less sensitive. And finally, because the vagina shrinks as estrogen decreases, it doesn't expand as much during intercourse, which may make intercourse less comfortable, especially because it is less lubricated.

Surgical Menopause

Surgical menopause is the result of a bilateral oophorectomy (the removal of both ovaries before natural menopause). Surgical menopause can also be the result of ovarian failure following a hysterectomy or following cancer therapy, such as chemotherapy or radiation treatments. A bilateral oophorectomy is often done in conjunction with a hysterectomy, or sometimes as a single procedure, when ovarian cancer is suspected, for example. In this section, I refer to menopause symptoms instead of "signs" or "changes," because menopause, in this case, is medically induced, rather than a natural occurrence.

Bilateral Oophorectomy Symptoms

If you've had your ovaries removed after menopause, you won't be in "surgical menopause." You won't feel any hormonal differences in your body, although you may experience some structural problems. If you've had your ovaries removed before you've reached natural menopause, you'll wake up from your surgery in *post*menopause. Once the ovaries are removed, your body immediately stops producing estrogen and progesterone. Your FSH will skyrocket in an attempt to "make contact" with ovaries that no longer exist. Unlike women who go through menopause naturally, women wake up after a bilateral oophorectomy in immediate estrogen "withdrawal." It's that sudden: One day you have a normal menstrual cycle, and the next, you have none whatsoever. This can cause you to become understandably more depressed, but you'll also *feel* the physical symptoms of estrogen loss far more intensely than a woman in natural menopause. That means that your vagina will be *extremely* dry, your hot flashes will feel like sudden violent heat waves that will be very disturbing to your system, and, of course, your periods will cease altogether, instead of tapering off naturally. The period that you had prior to your surgery will have been your last, so you won't even experience pre- or perimeno-pause, just postmenopause. That means that you'll need to begin estrogen replacement therapy (ERT) *immediately* following surgery to prevent these sudden symptoms of menopause. As you will soon discover, if you no longer have your uterus, you'll be on estrogen only, or unopposed estrogen. If you still have your uterus, you'll be placed on estrogen and progesterone hormone replacement therapy (HRT), for the reasons explained in the HRT/ERT section (pages 31–37). Any short-term menopausal symptoms will be alleviated by HRT/ERT. Prior to going on HRT/ERT, your doctor will perform a vaginal smear and a blood test to detect your FSH levels, which will tell him or her how much estrogen you need. Dosages will vary from woman to woman, so don't compare notes with your friends and wonder why "she's taking only X amount" when you're taking Y amount. ERT and HRT are discussed later in the chapter.

If you've just had one ovary removed

If the blood supply leading to your ovary was not damaged during your surgery then you should still be able to produce enough estrogen for your body. If you begin to go into ovarian failure, the symptoms will depend on how fast the ovary is failing; you may experience symptoms more akin to natural menopause, or you may experience sudden symptoms, mirroring the surgical menopause experience.

Ovarian Failure Resulting From Cancer Therapy

Chemotherapy and radiation treatments that involve the pelvic area may throw your ovaries into menopause. As previously mentioned, you may experience a more gradual menopausal process, or you may be overwhelmed by sudden symptoms of menopause. This depends on what kind of therapy you've received and the speed at which your ovaries are failing. Before you undergo your cancer treatment, discuss how the treatments will affect your ovaries and what menopausal symptoms you can expect.

Long-term Effects Of Estrogen Loss: Postmenopausal Changes

The long-term effects of estrogen loss have to do with traditional signs of "aging." One of the key reasons why women will choose HRT or ERT is to slow down or even reverse these changes. It's important to keep in mind that the long term effects of estrogen loss will not immediately set in after menopause. These changes are subtle and happen over several years. Even women who experience severe menopausal changes will not wake up to find that they've suddenly aged overnight; these changes occur gradually whether you experience surgical or natural menopause.

Skin Changes

As estrogen decreases, skin, as does the vagina, tends to lose its elasticity; it too becomes thinner because it is no longer able to retain as much water. Sweat and oil glands also produce less moisture, which is what causes the skin to gradually dry, wrinkle, and sag.

Good moisturizers and skin care will certainly help to keep your skin more elastic, but there is one known factor that aggravates and speeds up your skin's natural aging process, damaging the skin even more: *the sun*. If you cut down your sun exposure, you can dramatically reduce visible aging of your skin. Period. The bad news is that much of the sun's damage on our skin is cumulative from many years of exposure. In fact, many researchers believe that when it comes to visible signs of aging, *estrogen loss is only a small factor*. For example, it's known that ultraviolet rays break down collagen and elastin fibers in the skin, which cause it to break down and sag. This is also what puts us at risk for skin cancer, the most notorious of which is melanoma, one of the most aggressive and malignant of all cancers.

Other sun-related problems traditionally linked to estrogen loss are what we call "liver spots"—light brown or tan splotches that develop on the face, neck, and hands as we age. These spots have *nothing* to do with the liver; they are sunspots and are caused by sun exposure. In fact, they are sometimes the result of HRT, known in this case as *hyperpigmentation*.

Currently, dermatologists are recommending sunblocks with a minimum of SPF 15. In fact, sun damage is so widespread in our population that today sunblock is usually part of all North American women's daily cosmetic routine; women will put it on as regularly as a daily moisturizer.

Hormone Replacement Therapy

Hormone replacement therapy (HRT) refers to estrogen *and* progestin, which is a factory-made progestin, given to women after menopause who still have their uterus to prevent the lining from overgrowing and becoming cancerous. Estrogen replacement therapy (ERT) refers to estrogen only, which is given to women after surgical menopause who no longer have a uterus. Both HRT and ERT are designed to replace the estrogen lost after menopause, and hence:

1. Prevent or even reverse the long-term consequences of estrogen loss. The only proven long-term benefit of HRT is that it can help to preserve bone loss and reduce the incidence of fractures. Until July 2001, it was believed that HRT protected women from cardiovascular disease, but this is no longer considered true. In women who are at higher risk of breast cancer, HRT was always believed to be risky; now it is believed that it may trigger breast cancer in low-risk women.

2. Treat the short-term discomforts of menopause, such as the hot flashes and vaginal dryness. This is all still true, and you can discuss with your doctor how long she or he recommends you stay on HRT before it becomes risky.

If you decide, once you weigh the benefits and risks, to be treated with conventional HRT and/or ERT, you have the choice of using it as either a short- or a long-term therapy.

Being a slave to the medical system

An obvious, but under-reported, risk of HRT is that it forces you into another continuous cycle: one of constant doctor visits and tests. And each time you go to your doctor, you "risk" some sort of invasive procedure or referral for invasive tests. For example, women on HRT are more likely to be prescribed the following tests or medications:

➣ Blood tests for hormone levels.

➣ Diuretics for fluid retention.

➣ Ponstan, aspirin, or other analgesics for uterine cramps.

➣ Endometrial biopsies to check the endometrium.

➣ D&C (dilation and curettage) for bleeding.

➣ Baseline mammograms before starting therapy and regular mammograms thereafter.

➣ Visits for repeat prescriptions of hormones at least every six months.

Women who are not on HRT are not burdened by as many tests, visits, and other procedures. Do these increased doctor visits save lives because they offer early detection of many serious diseases? Critics of HRT argue that women are paying a higher price for their dependency on the medical system, and are burdened with too much monitoring and early detection.

The Forms of HRT and ERT

You can take estrogen in a number of ways. The most common estrogen product uses a synthesis of various estrogens that are derived from the urine of pregnant horses. That way the estrogen mimics nature more accurately. Estrogen replacement comes in either pills, patches (transdermal), or vaginal creams. Other common, synthetic forms of estrogen include micronized estradiol, ethinyl estradiol, esterified estrogen, and quinestrol.

As a short-term therapy, you may only need the vaginal cream to help with vaginal dryness or bladder problems. When estrogen is in patch or cream form, it goes directly to the bloodstream, bypassing the liver; this form of estrogen was previously discouraged to some women because it was not considered to have any protection against heart disease. But in light of the recent risk of heart disease with conventional formulations of HRT, the patch may pose no long-term harm, and you may want to discuss whether this is an option for more long-term use. Some women also have an allergic reaction to the skin patch and get a rash. If you're one of them, you can investigate taking the estrogen in other forms.

Finally, you can also have estrogen injected. Each shot lasts three to six weeks, but this is expensive and inconvenient because the dosages aren't as flexible with doses. Estrogen gel containing estradiol is now being used in some parts of the world, though it is not yet available in North America. The gel is spread over a wide area of the abdomen every second day. The problem women have encountered with this method is a variation in levels of absorption each time the gel is applied.

What About Progestin?

This is the synthetic version of progesterone that is found in all combination oral contraceptives. Progesterone receptors do not recognize progestin, and will not transport it to the cells. This may account for many of the progestin-related side effects that mimic premenstrual syndrome (PMS). The most common progestins include: Provera, Amen, Cretab, and Cycrin (all brand names of medroxyprogesterone acetate); Duralutin, Gesterol L.A., Hylutin, Hyprogest 250 (all brand names of hydroxyprogesterone caproate); Norlutate, Norgestrel, Aygestin (all brand names for norethindrone acetate); Norlutin (norethindrone); and Magace (Megestrol acetate). Micronor, Nor-Q.D., and Ovrette are brand name progestins on the market.

Progestins are taken in separate tablets along with estrogen. Together, the estrogen and progestin you take is called HRT. HRT can be administered two ways: *cyclically* or *continuously*. Taking HRT cyclically is very similar to taking an oral contraceptive (OC) because the hormones more closely mirror a natural cycle. The first day you start is considered day "1" of your mock "cycle." You take estrogen from day 1 to day 25; you then add the progesterone from day 14 to day 25. Then you stop all pills and bleed for two or three days—just as you would on a combination OC. This vaginal bleeding is called "withdrawal bleeding," which is lighter and shorter than a normal menstrual period, lasting only two or three days. In fact, if the bleeding is heavy or prolonged for some reason, this is a warning that something's not right, and you should see your doctor.

In addition, you may experience "breakthrough bleeding"— spotting during the first three weeks after you begin HRT. This kind of bleeding is again, similar to what happens on a combination OC. This bleeding usually goes away after a few months but should be reported nonetheless. You may need to switch to a lower dose of estrogen or take a higher dose of your progestin. Once your mini-period of withdrawal bleeding is finished, you simply start the cycle again. Many women can't tolerate cyclical HRT because they feel as though they should be *rid* of their periods by now and not have to deal with pads and tampons ever again. However, it is believed that cyclical HRT offers slightly better heart protection.

When HRT is taken continuously, you simply take one estrogen pill and one progestin pill each day. When you do it this way, the progesterone *counteracts* the estrogen; no uterine lining is built up, so there's no withdrawal bleeding that needs to happen.

The appropriate dosages

Every woman requires a different dosage of estrogen and progestin. But you will always be placed on the *lowest* possible dosage of either one, and may have the dosage increased gradually if necessary. If your estrogen dosage is too high, you'll experience side effects similar to those seen with oral contraceptives (headaches, bloating, and so on).

So before you determine how much estrogen you'll need, it's crucial to first determine how much your body is *still* producing; this really depends on your weight, estrogen loss discomforts, and a hundred other things.

Common side effects

If you're taking *cyclical* progestins with your estrogen because you still have your uterus, bleeding is *not* a side effect! The whole point of adding progestin to your estrogen is to trigger withdrawal bleeding and get your uterine lining routinely shed. However, if you're taking continuous progestins with your estrogen, bleeding is not the norm and should be checked into.

Common side effects of estrogen will include fluid retention, because estrogen will decrease the amount of salt and water excreted by kidneys, which is retained by legs, breasts, and feet which can swell. Because of the fluid retention, you may weigh more, but you will not you might also gain weight.

Nausea is another common side effect, also seen with oral contraceptives. This happens during the first two or three months of your therapy, and should just disappear on its own. Some women find that taking their dosages at night (for pills) may remedy this. Decreasing the dosage is also an option.

Some other side effects reported include headaches, skin color changes called *melasma* on face, more cervical mucous secretion, liquid secretion from breasts, change in curvature of cornea, jaundice, loss of scalp hair, and itchiness. Again, these side effects vary and depend on the brand you're taking, the dosage, your medical history, and so on.

Are You an HRT or ERT Candidate?

In light of the recent shadow cast over HRT, clearly it is not for everyone. Here's a guide that may help you make the decision for short-term use of HRT:

> ➤ Do you suffer from severe hot flashes that don't respond to natural remedies, outlined later in this chapter?

> ➤ Are your vaginal changes causing painful intercourse, urinary tract infections, or vaginitis, which does not respond to natural remedies, such as more stimulation of the clitoris during sex, or sexual lubricants?

Using HRT in the long term may still be an option if *you want protection from developing osteoporosis.* Again, ERT or HRT will lower your risk. (But so will exercise and a high-calcium diet.) There are now bone-building drugs that are alternatives to HRT you can discuss with your doctor.

Women who shouldn't be on ERT or HRT

> ➤ Women with (a history of) endometrial cancer should not be on unopposed estrogen (ERT). Again, if you still have a uterus, you'll be placed on HRT (estrogen and progesterone), which lowers your cancer risk anyway.

➤ Women with breast cancer, with a history of breast cancer, or who are considered at high risk for breast cancer.

➤ Women who have had a stroke. Neither ERT nor HRT is recommended.

➤ Women who have a blood-clotting disorder. Neither ERT nor HRT is recommended.

➤ Women with undiagnosed vaginal bleeding. Neither therapy is recommended.

➤ Women with liver dysfunction. You can be on the estrogen patch or vaginal cream to relieve your menopausal discomforts but you shouldn't take any pills orally.

Women who may benefit more from HRT/ERT

Discuss whether you're a candidate for HRT, given its protective effects against osteoporosis and colon cancer. However, you may need to think twice if you have the following *other* conditions:

➢ Sickle cell disease.

➢ High blood pressure.

➢ Migraines.

➢ Uterine fibroids.

➢ A history of benign breast conditions such as cysts or fibroadenomas.

➢ Endometriosis.

➢ Seizures.

➢ Gallbladder disease.

➢ A family history of breast cancer.

➢ A past or current history of smoking.

What to Eat

This section gives you plenty of ideas if you're wondering about herbal remedies, nourishing and toning herbs during perimenopause and after menopause. The variety in this section is there to give you choices, not to suggest that you must try everything.

Many of these can be taken as teas or oral capsules; please consult your herbal retailer or an herbalist (often on staff at heath food stores, for example), for the best available format. It frequently depends on which brands you herbal retailer has in stock.

How to Have "Safe Herbs"

1. Buy herbs that are labeled with the botanical name specific to only one plant. For example, "sage" can refer to at least 5 plants in 5 different areas, but *Salvia officinalis* means garden sage only.

2. Introduce yourself to one herb at a time, and try to learn all you can about your "new herb." That means experimenting: Does it work best at different times of day, or with certain foods or other herbs you know well?

3. Herbs can be "tonic" (maintenance herbs) or "active" (sedating or stimulating). Tonic herbs include: birch, black cohosh, blackstrap molasses, chaste tree, dandelion, Dong Quai/Dang Gui, echinacea, false unicorn, ginseng, hawthorn, horsetail, lady's mantle, motherwort, peony, sarsaparilla, spikenard, wild yam and yellow dock. "Active" herbs include, catnip, cinnamon, ginger, hops, licorice, myrrh, passion flower, poplar, primrose, sage, skullcap, uva ursi, valerian, vervain, willow, and wintergreen.

4. Herbs can also be toxic in high quantities. Toxic herbs include cayenne, cotton root, goldenseal, liferoot, poke root, rue, sweet clover (Melilot), and wormseed.

For Irregular Cycles

➤ **Raspberry leaf.** Best as an infusion (see Table 1.1). Nourishes the ovaries as well as the uterus. Helps with erratic periods.

➤ **Dong Quai/Dang Gui compound.** As a tincture, this warms, regulates, and gently heals the entire reproductive system. Especially useful if your irregular cycles are accompanied with PMS. (*Note:* Dong Quai can aggravate fibroids.)

➤ **Liferoot blossoms.** As a tincture, five drops taken daily helps tone the reproductive-hormones, ovaries, uterus, adrenals, liver, and pituitary gland.

➤ **Vitex.** As a tincture, this helps with irregular periods. Use one "dropperful" in a small glass of water two or three times daily for xi to eight weeks after every irregular period.

➤ **Cinnamon bark** (*Cinnamon zeylanicum*). This invigorates the blood, helps regulate the menstrual cycle, and helps with very heavy flows (a.k.a. "flooding"). As an infusion, sip a cup/250 ml of infusion, use five to 10 drops of tincture once or twice a day, gnaw on a cinnamon stick, or simply sprinkle cinnamon on everything.

For Heavy Flows

If you're coping with very heavy menstrual flows (a.k.a. "flooding") then it's important to consume roughly 2 mg iron from herbs or foods while the bleeding persists. This will help to prevent anemia. Iron is best in small doses throughout the day, rather than in one big gulp. Coffee, black tea, soy protein, egg yolks, bran, and calcium supplements more than 250 mg can also impair iron absorption. Bleeding can be aggravated by aspirin, Midol, and larger doses of ascorbic acid (vitamin C supplements) because they thin the blood. In general, foods rich in bioflavonoids and carotene will help with blood loss.

Herbs

> **Dandelion leaves.** This is the best source of useable iron, containing roughly 30 grams of iron per ounce.

> **Yellow dock root.** An alcohol or vinegar tincture is best Twenty drops of alcohol tincture or 3 teaspoons/15 ml vinegar, taken in tea or water, gives you 1 mg iron to the blood.

> **Lady's Mantle** *(Alchemilla vulgaris)*.The alchemical weed, controlled menstrual hemorrhage in virtually all of more than 300 women in a recent study.

> **Wild yam root.** As a tincture, 20-30 drops daily for the two weeks before your period can help reduce flow.

Estrogen Herbs

The following herbs help promote estrogen production, stabilize infrequent periods, and may reduce the severity of estrogen-loss discomforts:

> Alfalfa and red clover flowers/leaves.

> Black cohosh roots.

> Hops (female flowers).

> Licorice roots.

> Sage leaves.

> Sweet briar hips or leaf buds.

> Pomegranate seeds.

> Any herb containing flavonoids.

Progesterone Herbs

The following herbs help promote progesterone production, and help stabilize too-frequent periods:

- ➤ Chaste tree/vitex berries.
- ➤ Sarsaparilla roots.
- ➤ Wild yam roots.
- ➤ Yarrow flowers and leaves.

Phytoestrogens

The following are plant estrogens, which may help with a myriad of menopausal discomforts:

- ➤ Agave *(Agave Americana)*. One dose is 1/4-1 teaspoon/1-5 ml of juice of the leaves.
- ➤ Alfalfa.
- ➤ Amerikanerischer Schneeball (also available as Schneeball).
- ➤ Black cohosh.
- ➤ Black currant.
- ➤ Black haw.
- ➤ Bockshornklee.
- ➤ Casses *(Ribes nigrm)*.
- ➤ Chaste tree *(Vitex agnus castus)*.
- ➤ Cimicifuga *(Cimicifuga racemosa)*.
- ➤ Cramp bark.
- ➤ Dandelion.
- ➤ Devil's club *(Chamalirium luteum)*.
- ➤ Dong Quai/Dang Gui *(Angelica sinensis)*.
- ➤ Fenugreek *(good for hot flashes)*.

- Garden Sage *(Salvia officinalis)*. Good for night sweats.
- Gemeines Kreuzkraut.
- Ginseng *(Panax quinquefolium)*.
- Groundsel.
- Hopfen.
- Hops.
- Houblon grimpant *(Humulus lupulus)*.
- Licorice. (*Note:* This can be toxic in high doses, causing high blood pressure and water retention.)
- Liferoot *(Senecio aureus)*.
- Lowenzahn.
- Luzerne.
- Luzerne cultivee *(Medicago sativa)*.
- Motherwort *(Leonurus cardiaca. Good for night sweats)*.
- Nettle *(Urtica dioica* or *U. Urens)*.
- Peony. Frequently combines with Dong Quai/Dang Gui.
- Pomegranate (Punica granatum). These seeds pack 1.7 grams of estrone for every 3 ounces. Just eat the seeds instead of spitting them out when you consume the fruit. Or make them into a "smoothie" in the blender. You can also rind them and infuse in oil to make your own estrogen cream.
- Raspberry *(Rubus species)*.
- Red Clover *(Trifolium praetense)*.
- Rose "family" (Raspberry, strawberry, sweet briar, and hawthorn). Rose hips are an excellent source of flavonoids.
- Sarsaparilla *(Smilax officinalis* or *S. regelii)*. Jamaican is considered best, with Mexican and Honduran following closely.
- Saw palmetto *(Serenoa serrulata)*.
- Schlangenwurzel.

➤ Schwarze or Schwarze Johannisbeere.

➤ Senecon Commun *(Senecio vulgaris)*. Her sister plant is Jacob's Groundsel. Jakobskraut Senecon Jacobee *(Senecio Jacobea)* are closely related to liferoot.

➤ Sweet briar or dog rose, Hagrose, Eglantier *(Rosa canina or R. pendulina)*.

➤ Viorne obier *(Viburnum opulis)* or Viburnum *(Viburnum prunifolium)*.

➤ Wild yam *(Dioscorea villosa* and all 500 related species). Progesterone cream derived from wild yam had been shown to reverse osteoporosis.

➤ Yarrow *(Achillea milefolium)*.

For Hot Flashes

Hot flashes deplete your body of vitamins B and C, magnesium, and potassium. Red clover or oatstraw infusions will replace these lost nutrients. Taking vitamin B (B2, B6, and B12), vitamin C, and vitamin E supplements is also helpful.

Herbal remedies

It's suggested that you combine one of the following to help reduce the severity of hot flashes:

1. A "cooling" herb such as chickweed, elder flower, violet oatstraw, mint, seaweeds, all parts of the mallows *(Malva species)*, and the flowers and leaves of any hibiscus.

2. A liver-nourishing herb, such as dandelion, yellow dock, Lowenzahn *(Taraxacum officinale)* root, Ho Shou Wu *(Polygonum multiflorum)* root, also sold as Fo-ti-tieng; or milk thistle *(Syllibum)*, chicory *(Cichorium intybus)*, oatstraw.

3. A plant estrogen, such as black cohosh. (See previous pages for a list of phyestrogens.)

How to Move

This section suggests activities, exercises, or specific movements to help reduce the severity of estrogen-loss discomforts.

Exercise

Any kind of physical exercise can decrease hot flashes because it increases endorphin levels, which immediately counteract hot flashes. The recommended "dose" is 20 minutes three times per week.

For Hot Flashes

➤ Sit on the floor with knees bent. Hold the point below your middle toe with your right hand, maintaining steady pressure for one to three minutes.

➤ Move your right hand to the point behind your ankle bone. Again, hold with steady pressure for one to three minutes and repeat both exercises on the left side.

➤ With your left hand, hold the point on your right hand just outside of the ring finger. Repeat on the left side.

For hot flashes, excessive menstrual bleeding, and other disturbances of the reproductive tract:

➤ Lie on your back on the floor, with your knees bent and feet on the floor. Place a chair behind your head (seat facing you). Place a knotted towel between the shoulder blades on the spine and hold for one to three minutes.

➤ With arms crossed across the chest, press your thumbs against the insides of your arms above the elbows. Hold for one to three minutes.

➤ Move your left hand to the point at the base of the sternum or breastbone. Hold with steady pressure while you move your right hand to the point where the spine meets the back of the skull. Hold for one to three minutes.

- Interlace your fingers and let them rest below your breasts. Press the tips of your fingers into your chest area with steady pressure. Hold for one to three minutes.

- Slide the knotted towel downwards until it rests below your waistline. Apply steady pressure to the tailbone with your right hand and to the tip of the pubic bone with your left hand. Hold for one to three minutes.

- While on your back, gently roll one, then the other shoulder inwards, shortening the distance between your shoulder blades. Bring your knees to your chest, supporting your hips with your hands. Gently bring your legs up and over your body until they are resting on the chair behind you. Lift the spine by stretching the back muscles as much as possible. Breathe deeply and hold.

- While on your back with your knees bent, gently roll one, then the other shoulder inwards, shortening the distance between your shoulder blades. With hands supporting the hips, slowly raise your pelvis toward the ceiling. Breathe deeply, feeling the muscles contract along the front of your body. Release.

Aromatherapy

The following essential oils can help ease hot flashes; use in a bath or diffuser:

- Calamus/sweet flag.
- Basil.
- Thyme.

Miscellaneous

- Use a hand-held fan.
- Use cologne, which is mostly alcohol and cooling.
- Bathe using 3 ounces/80 ml rubbing alcohol.

For Irregular Periods

Both regular orgasms (through self or partnered stimulation) and pelvic floor exercises can help maintain regular periods.

Table 1.1
How to Make an Herbal Infusion

An infusion is a strong tea or a brew that does not keep longer than about 3 days. An infusion is a large amount of dried (not fresh) herbs or plants brewed for a long time. You can use a sauce or a teapot to make an infusion. You drink the infusion either hot, room temperature, or chilled. You can sweeten them with sugar, honey, sugar substitutes, and even add milk. You can bathe in infusions as well or use them as rinses for your hair or skin.

Directions:

➤ When using roots or bark: Use about 1 ounce (30 grams) to 500 ml water and steep for eight hours.

➤ When using leaves: Use about 1 ounce (30 grams) to one quart of water and steep for four hours.

➤ When using flowers: Use about 1 ounce (30 grams) to one quart of water and steep for two hours.

➤ When using seeds/berries: Use about 1 ounce (30 grams) to one quart water and steep for 30 minutes.

Table 1.2
How to Make an Herbal Tincture

An herbal tincture means that you are steeping fresh plants in alcohol (not vinegar), which is what makes them heavily alkaline. Tinctures can be made with fresh plants and herbs or dried roots, seeds, and berries.

The best steps to a good tincture:

1. Coarsely chop fresh or dried plant. Do not wash.

2. Put the choppings into a glass jar and fill the jar with 100-proof vodka.

3. Seal the jar tightly and label it with the date and the name of your plant.

4. Open in six weeks. It can stay for at least a year.

Proportions for Fresh Plants:
   1 ounce (30 grams) of fresh plants per 1 ounce of vodka (30 ml) is the norm

Proportions for Dried Plants:
   1 ounce (30 grams) of dried plant material in five ounces (150 ml) vodka

Your Heart of Hearts

Just sing along—you must know the words by now: Heart disease is currently the number-one cause of death in postmenopausal women; more women die of heart disease than of lung cancer or breast cancer. Half of all North Americans who die from heart attacks each year are women. But heart disease doesn't just refer to heart attacks; it refers to strokes and a whole gamut of problems due to poor circulation, known in clinical circles as *peripheral vascular disease*, or more plainly "blood circulation disease."

One of the reasons for such high death rates from heart attacks among women is medical ignorance: Most studies looking at heart disease excluded women, which led to a myth that more men than women die of heart disease. The truth is that more *men* die of heart attacks *before* age 50; more *women* die of heart attacks *after* age 50, as a direct result of estrogen loss. Moreover, women who have had oophorectomies (removal of the ovaries) prior to natural menopause increase their risk of a heart attack *eight times*. Because more women work outside the home than ever before, a number of experts cite stress as a huge contributing factor to increased rates of heart disease in women.

Another problem is that women have different symptoms than men when it comes to heart disease, and so the "typical" warning signs we know about in men—angina, or chest pains—are often never present in women. In fact, chest pains in women are almost never related to heart disease. When symptoms of heart disease are not "male," many women are sent home to die, told that their heart attack is "stress."

This chapter will outline all the modifiable risk factors for heart disease and discuss the warning signs of a heart attack—in *women*. What to Eat (page 67) explains heart smart diets and all of the heart smart herbs available, while How To Move (page 79) explains aerobic vs. anaerobic activities, as well postures that improve circulation and oxygen flow to the heart.

Who's at Risk for Heart Disease?

There are a number of modifiable risk factors that can predispose you to heart disease. That means risks that can be modified, or altered, versus risks you can't change, such as your age or your family history.

Smoking

Roughly half a million North Americans die of smoking-related illnesses each year. That's 20 percent of *all* deaths from *all* causes. We already know that smoking causes lung cancer. But did you know that smokers are also *twice* as likely to develop heart disease? Factor in other risk factors, such as estrogen loss, and you're at enormous risk for heart disease if you're a postmenopausal smoker. A single cigarette affects your body within seconds, increasing heart rate, blood pressure, and the demand for oxygen. The greater the demand for oxygen (because of constricted blood vessels and carbon monoxide, a by-product of cigarettes), the greater the risk of heart disease.

Lesser-known long-term effects of smoking include a lowering of HDL, or "good" cholesterol, and damage to the lining of blood vessel walls, which paves the way for arterial plaque formation. In addition to increasing your risk for lung cancer and heart disease, smoking can lead to stroke, peripheral vascular disease, and a host of other cancers.

Quitting smoking

The symptoms of nicotine withdrawal begin within a few hours and peak at 24–48 hours after quitting. You may experience anxiety, irritability, hostility, restlessness, insomnia, and anger. However, take a look at some of the things you'll gain by quitting smoking:

> ➢ Decreased risk of heart disease.

> ➢ Decreased risk of cancer (that includes lung, esophagus, mouth, throat, pancreas, kidney, bladder, and cervix).

> ➢ Lower heart rate and blood pressure.

> ➢ Deceased risk of lung disease (bronchitis, emphysema).

> ➢ Relaxation of blood vessels.

> ➢ Improved sense of smell and taste.

> ➢ Healthier teeth.

> ➢ Fewer wrinkles.

Not everyone can quit "cold turkey," although it's a strategy that many have used successfully. (Some "cold turkey" quitters report that keeping one package of cigarettes within reach lessons anxiety.) Here are some other smoking cessation methods:

➤ **Behavioral counseling:** Behavioral counseling, either group or individual, can raise the rate of abstinence to 20–25 percent. This approach to smoking cessation aims to change the mental processes of smoking, reinforce the benefits of nonsmoking, and teach skills to help the smoker avoid the urge to smoke.

➤ **Nicotine Gum:** Nicotine (Nicorette) gum is now available over the counter in Canada and the United States. It works as an aid to help you quit smoking by reducing nicotine cravings and withdrawal symptoms. Nicotine gum helps you wean yourself from nicotine by allowing you to gradually decrease the dosage until you stop using it altogether, a process that usually takes about 12 weeks. The only disadvantage with this method is that it caters to the oral and addictive aspects of smoking (that is, rewarding the "urge" to smoke with a dose of nicotine).

➤ **Nicotine Patch:** Transdermal nicotine, or the "patch" (Habitrol, Nicoderm, Nicotrol), doubles abstinence rates in former smokers. Most brands are now available over the counter in both Canada and the United States. Each morning, a new patch is applied to a different area of dry, clean, hairless skin and left on for the day. Some patches are designed to be worn a full 24 hours. However, the constant supply of nicotine to the bloodstream sometimes causes very vivid or disturbing dreams. You can also expect to feel a mild itching, burning, or tingling at the site of the patch when it is first applied. The nicotine patch works best when it is worn for at least seven to 12 weeks, with a gradual decrease in (nicotine) strength. Many smokers find it effective because it allows them to tackle the psychological addiction to smoking before they are forced to deal with physical symptoms of withdrawal.

➤ **Nicotine Inhaler:** The nicotine inhaler (Nicotrol Inhaler) delivers nicotine orally via inhalation from a plastic tube. Its success rate is about 28 percent, similar to that of nicotine gum. It's available by prescription only in the United States, and has yet to make its debut in Canada. As does nicotine gum, the inhaler mimics smoking behavior by responding to each craving or "urge" to smoke, a feature that has both advantages and disadvantages to the smoker who wants to get over the physical symptoms of withdrawal. The nicotine inhaler should be used for a period of 12 weeks.

➤ **Nicotine Nasal Spray:** As do nicotine gum and the nicotine patch, the nasal spray reduces craving and withdrawal symptoms, allowing smokers to cut back gradually. One squirt delivers about 1 mg nicotine. In three clinical trials involving 730 patients, 31–35 percent were not smoking at six months. This compares to an average of 12–15 percent of smokers who were able to quit unaided. The nasal spray has a couple of advantages over the gum and the patch: nicotine is rapidly absorbed across the nasal membranes, providing a kick that is more like the real thing; and the prompt onset of action plus a flexible dosing schedule benefits heavier smokers. Because the nicotine reaches your bloodstream so quickly, nasal sprays do have a greater potential for addiction than the slower-acting gum and patch. Nasal sprays are not yet available for use in Canada.

➤ **Bupropion:** Bupropion (Zyban) is appropriate for patients who have been unsuccessful using nicotine replacement. Formerly prescribed as an antidepressant, Bupropion was "discovered" by accident: Researchers knew that quitting smokers were often depressed, and so they began experimenting with the drug as a means to fight depression, not addiction. Bupropion reduces the withdrawal symptoms associated with smoking cessation and can be used in conjunction with nicotine replacement therapy. Researchers suspect that Bupropion works directly in the brain to disrupt the addictive power of nicotine by affecting the same chemical neurotransmitters (or "messengers") in the brain, such as dopamine, that nicotine does. The pleasurable aspect of addictive drugs such as nicotine and cocaine is triggered by the release of dopamine. Smoking floods the brain with dopamine. *The New England Journal of Medicine* published the results of a study of more than 600 smokers taking Bupropion. At the end of treatment, 44 percent of those who took the highest dose of the drug (300 mg) were not smoking, compared to 19 percent of the group who took a placebo. By the end of one year, 23 percent of the 300 mg group and 12 percent of the placebo group were still smoke-free. Using Zyban *with* nicotine replacement therapy seems to improve the quit rate a bit further. Four-week quit rates from the study were 23 percent for placebo, 36 percent for the patch, 49 percent for Zyban, and 58 percent for the combination of Zyban and the patch.

➤ **Alternative therapies:** Hypnosis, meditation, and acupuncture have helped some smokers quit. In the case of hypnosis and meditation, sessions may be private or part of a group smoking-cessation program.

Obesity

If you weigh 20 percent more than your ideal weight for your height and age, you're technically obese. It's not the weight that's the problem; it's the health conditions that usually accompany that weight, such as Type 2 diabetes, high blood pressure, and high cholesterol, which can put you at risk for heart disease.

Sedentary Lifestyle

Women who are physically active have a 60–75 percent lower risk of heart disease that inactive women. See How to Move (page 79) for more details.

High Cholesterol

Cholesterol is a whitish, waxy fat made in vast quantities by the liver. That's why liver or other organ meats are high in cholesterol! Cholesterol is needed to make hormones as well as cell membranes. If you have high cholesterol, the excess cholesterol in your blood can lead to narrowed arteries, which, in men, can definitely lead to a heart attack. Saturated fat, discussed in detail in What to Eat (page 67), is often a culprit when it comes to high cholesterol, but sometimes the highest levels of cholesterol are due to a genetic defect in the liver, which may not be modifiable.

The story of women and high cholesterol is still unfolding. You see, when it comes to high cholesterol, newer research is showing that it is not as much of a risk factor for heart disease in women as it is for men. If you've already suffered a heart attack, then following a low saturated-fat diet will help to lower the "bad cholesterol" (the LDL, or low-density lipoproteins levels) and raise your HDL (high density lipoproteins, or "good cholesterol") levels. Similarly, if you smoke, have high blood pressure, are obese, have Type 2 diabetes, or have a family history of heart disease, following the low-fat/lower cholesterol diet will help improve your health, too.

But for healthy women older than 65 years of age, with higher than "normal" cholesterol, who don't smoke, and have no other risk factors for heart disease other than age, there's no clear benefit to lowering cholesterol, or even worrying about it. We know, for example that very few premenopausal women with high cholesterol ever develop heart disease, leading researchers to conclude that other factors are more significant for women than high cholesterol. So, although high cholesterol is *definitely* linked to male heart disease, it is *not* definitely linked to female heart disease, and, in fact, may not even be a big deal. So, most physicians will recommend a low-fat diet to women with *other* risk factors for heart disease because, in a nutshell, it can't hurt and will improve other health problems.

The current guidelines most physicians in North America follow when managing cholesterol in women are to encourage women over 20 to begin a lower cholesterol (meaning, low saturated-fat diet; see What to Eat, page 67) if their cholesterol levels are 200 mg/dL or more. If you have very low good or HDL cholesterol levels (less than 35 mg/dL), then your doctor should measure the bad or LDL cholesterol levels; an LDL level of less than 130 mg/dL is desirable. LDL levels of 130–159 mg/dL are borderline-high. Levels of 160 mg/dL or more are high. A low saturated-fat diet will probably be the recommendation. If you already have heart disease, you should aim to have LDL readings of about 100 mg/dL or less, which is lower than the guidelines for women without heart disease. In this case, your doctor may recommend that, in addition to a low saturated fat diet, you also take a cholesterol-lowering drug, discussed further on.

Cholesterol levels are checked through a simple blood test. You can also ask your pharmacist about the availability of home cholesterol tests.

If your blood cholesterol is between 200 and 239 mg/dl, as long as you don't smoke, are not obese, have normal blood pressure, are *pre*menopausal, and do not have a family history of heart disease, you're fine! A high "total cholesterol" reading should always be followed up with an HDL/LDL analysis.

Lowering cholesterol without drugs

Overall by modifying your diet (see What to Eat) and exercising (see How to Move), you'll probably be able to lower your cholesterol without taking any medication. Vitamin E has been shown to lower cholesterol, too, preventing the formation of arterial plaque. A 46-percent drop in the incidence of heart attack was reported in a study of 87,000 nurses taking vitamin E. On the basis of that study, doctors now recommend a dosage of 100 IV (international units) daily. As for vitamin C, we still don't know how much vitamin C is needed to reduce the risk of heart attack. Consumption of large amounts of vitamin C was associated with lower rates of coronary artery disease in an eight-year study at Brigham and Women's Hospital in Boston. Some experts recommend 10 mg or more per day. For more on heart-smart nutrients, see What to Eat.

Cholesterol-lowering drugs

For many, losing weight and modifying fat intake simply aren't enough to bring cholesterol levels down to optimal levels. You may be a candidate for one of the numerous cholesterol-lowering drugs that have hit the market in recent years. These medications, when combined with a low-fat, low-cholesterol diet, target the intestine, blocking food absorption, and/or the liver, where they interfere with the processing of cholesterol. These are strong drugs, however, and ought to be a last resort after really giving a low fat/low cholesterol diet a chance. You might be given a combination of cholesterol-lowering medications to try with a low cholesterol diet. It's important to ask about all side effects accompanying your medication because they can include gastrointestinal problems, allergic reactions, blood disorders, and depression. (One study, looking at male patients taking cholesterol-lowering drugs, noted an unusually high rate of suicide and accidental trauma among male subjects taking these medications.) There have not been enough studies on women taking these drugs to truly know how they interact with women's health conditions. At any rate, here's what is available as of this writing. Please note only the generic drug names are listed.

➤ **Niacin.** When taken properly, niacin is the best cholesterol treatment available. In 1986 the Coronary Drug Project (a National Institute of Health study) found that prolonged use of niacin significantly reduced mortality rates among heart attack victims. It has since become one of the most popular cholesterol-lowering drugs on the market. Niacin, a water-soluble vitamin B, can lower LDL by 30 percent and triglyceride levels by as much as 55 percent. It also increases HDL by about 35 percent. Also known as nicotinic acid, niacin must be taken in large doses (one to three mg/day) in order to be effective. Because the dosage is up to 76 times more than the recommended daily allowance, side effects are common. Many patients experience itching, flushing, and panic attacks. Switching to slow-release capsules, taking an aspirin 30 minutes before taking the medication, or taking it on a full stomach might help alleviate some of these symptoms. Niacin can aggravate both stomach ulcers and diabetes.

➤ **Statins.** Statins, such as "Mevacor" and "Zocar," hinder the liver's ability to produce cholesterol, keeping LDL levels to a minimum while increasing levels of HDL. When combined with the proper diet, statins can reduce your risk of death from heart disease by as much as 40 percent. However, certain lovastatins (that is, Zocar) have been known to cause liver damage, muscle pain, and weakness.

➤ **Cholestyramine.** Cholestyramine helps the body eliminate cholesterol through the gut. It is considered the safest of cholesterol-lowering drugs; it has also been around the longest. A National Institute of Health study in the early 1980s demonstrated that Cholestyramine decreases heart attack deaths by lowering cholesterol levels. In fact, for each 1-percent drop in the cholesterol levels of participants, there was a 2-percent drop in death rates. Pretty impressive when you consider the fact that the average decline in blood cholesterol was 25 percent. Although cholestyramine reduces LDL or bad cholesterol, it can sometimes raise triglyceride levels. It can also trigger a host of side effects, the most unpleasant of which is *really bad* gas. Cholestyramine interferes with the effectiveness of digitalis, diuretics, warfarin, fat-soluble vitamins, and beta-blockers. It can also lead to gallstones. Cholestyramine should be taken in the morning and at bedtime.

➤ **Gemfibrozil.** Gemfibrozil lowers cholesterol and triglyceride levels in the blood. The rate of coronary artery disease among 4,000 men with high cholesterol involved in a Finnish study dropped 34 percent. Gemfibrozil should be taken in 600 mg tablets twice daily.

➤ **Probucol.** Probucol can cut your LDL by as much as 15 percent, but it also lowers your HDL, or "good" cholesterol. Lately Probucol is generating new interest among doctors because it is also a powerful antioxidant. LDL creates arterial plaque through a change in its molecular make-up. This "change" is called oxidation, and an antioxidant such as Probucol can help to prevent it from happening.

➤ **Arginine.** Preliminary studies suggest that this amino acid may lower cholesterol levels and improve coronary blood flow by acting as an antioxidant and maintaining elasticity in blood vessel tissues. Arginine is currently available without a prescription.

➤ **Coenzyme Q10.** Japanese and European practitioners love this powerful antioxidant, but more studies are needed to prove its reputed effect on arterial plaque.

High Blood Pressure

About 12 percent of all North American adults suffer from hypertension, or high blood pressure. What exactly is blood pressure? The blood flows from the heart into the arteries (blood vessels), pressing against the artery walls. The simplest way to explain this is to think about a liquid-soap dispenser. When you want soap, you need to pump it out by pressing down on the little dispenser pump, the "heart" of the dispenser. The liquid soap is the "blood," and the little tube, through which the soap flows, is the "artery." The pressure that's exerted on the wall of the tube is therefore the "blood pressure."

When the tube is hollow and clean, you needn't pump very hard to get the soap; it comes out easily. But when the tubing in your dispenser gets narrower as a result of old, hardened, gunky liquid soap blocking the tube, you have to pump down much harder to get any soap, all the while increasing the force the soap exerts against the tube. Obviously, this is a simplistic explanation of a very complex problem, but essentiallyad the narrowing of the arteries, created by higher blood pressure, forces your heart to work harder to pump the blood. If this goes on too long, your heart muscle enlarges and becomes weaker, which can lead to a heart attack. Higher pressure can also weaken the walls of your blood vessels, which can cause a stroke.

The term hyper*tension* refers to the tension or force exerted on your artery walls. (Hyper means "too much," as in "too much tension.") Blood pressure is measured in two readings: X over Y. The X is the systolic pressure, which is the pressure that occurs during the heart's contraction. The Y is the diastolic pressure, which is the pressure that occurs when the heart rests between contractions. In "liquid soap" terms, the systolic pressure occurs when you press the pump down; the diastolic pressure occurs when you release your hand from the pump and allow it to rise back to its "resting" position.

Normal blood pressure readings are 120 over 80 (120/80). Readings of 140/90 or higher are generally considered borderline, although for some people this is still considered a normal reading. For the general population, 140/90 is "lecture time," when your doctor will begin to counsel you about dietary and lifestyle habits. By 160/100, many people are prescribed a hypertensive drug, which is designed to lower blood pressure.

Know the causes of high blood pressure

The most common causes of high blood pressure are obesity, inactivity, and stress. High blood pressure is also exacerbated by tobacco and alcohol consumption and too much sodium or salt in the diet. (People of African descent tend to be more salt-sensitive.)

If high blood pressure runs in the family, you're considered at greater risk of developing hypertension. High blood pressure can also be caused by kidney disorders or pregnancy (known as pregnancy-induced hypertension). Medications are also common culprits. Estrogen-containing medications (such as oral contraceptives), non-steroidal anti-inflammatory drugs (NSAIDs), such as ibuprofen, nasal decongestants, cold remedies, appetite suppressants, certain antidepressants, and other drugs, can all increase blood pressure. Be sure to check with your pharmacist.

How to lower your blood pressure without drugs

> ➤ Change your diet and begin exercising (see What to Eat and How to Move, pages 67 and 79 respectively).

> ➤ Limit alcohol consumption to no more than 2 oz. of liquor, 8 oz. of wine, or 24 oz. of beer per day, and lower still for "liver health."

> ➤ Limit your salt intake to about 1–1/2 teaspoons per day. Cut out all foods high in sodium, such as canned soups, pickles, soy sauce, and so on. Some canned soups contain 1,000 mg of sodium, for example. That's a lot!

> ➤ Increase your intake of calcium or dairy products and potassium (for example, bananas). Some still-unproven studies suggest that people with hypertension are calcium- and potassium-deficient.

> ➤ Lower your stress levels. Studies show that by lowering your stress, your blood pressure decreases (see further on).

Blood pressure-lowering drugs

If you can't lower your blood pressure through lifestyle changes, you may be a candidate for some of the following blood pressure-lowering drugs:

> ➤ **Diuretics.** Diuretics are the most commonly used blood pressure medication. Also known as water pills, diuretics work by flushing excess water and salt (often two to four pounds worth!) out of your system. But diuretics may actually increase the risk of heart attack by leaching potassium salts needed by the heart, and the heart may respond to blocked nerve signals by trying harder and harder, until it fails. Another common side effect of diuretic therapy is low potassium. Levels of potassium tend

to drop when diuretics replace the low-fat diet you've worked so hard to maintain. If you make sure not to substitute one therapy for another, diuretics will not affect your potassium levels. Other side effects include increased blood sugar and cholesterol levels.

➤ **Beta-blockers.** Beta-blockers alter the way hormones, such as adrenaline, control blood pressure. They slow the heart rate down by decreasing the strength of its contractions. Beta-blockers are most often used by young people and/or people with coronary artery disease. Possible side effects include fatigue and an increase in blood sugar and cholesterol levels.

➤ **Centrally acting agents.** These drugs act through centers in the brain to slow the heart rate and relax the blood vessels. Possible side effects include stuffy nose, dry mouth, and drowsiness.

➤ **Vasodilators.** Vasodilators dilate, or relax, the blood vessels, thereby reducing blood pressure.

➤ **Ace-inhibitors.** Ace-inhibitors lower blood pressure by preventing the formation of a hormone called angiotensin II, which causes the blood vessels to narrow. Ace-inhibitors are also used to treat heart failure. Possible side effects include cough and swelling of the face and tongue.

➤ **Alpha-blocking agents.** Alpha-blocking agents block the effects of noradrenaline, allowing the blood vessels to relax. Blood pressure decreases with treatment, as does cholesterol. You may also notice an increase in HDL, or "good" cholesterol. A possible side effect is blood pressure variation when standing versus reclining.

➤ **Calcium-channel blockers.** Calcium-channel blockers limit the amount of calcium entering the cells, allowing the muscles in the blood vessels to relax. Possible side effects include ankle swelling, flushing, constipation and indigestion.

Type 2 Diabetes

If you have Type 2 diabetes, your risk of a heart attack or stroke is at least four times greater than in the general population. In fact, Type 2 diabetes is referred to as "a heart attack about to happen." For more information about Type 2 diabetes complications, consult my book *THe Natural Woman's Guide to Living With the Complications of Diabetes* (New Page Books, 2003). Diabetes (McGraw-Hill, 2000).

The Role of Stress

Heart disease is also believed to be triggered by stress. Before you can look at what you can do to manage your stress, the first order of business is to understand what stress exactly is.

Generally, stress is defined as a negative emotional experience associated with biological changes that allow you to adapt to it. In response to stress, your adrenal glands pump out "stress hormones" that speed up your body: Your heart rate increases, and your blood sugar levels increase so that glucose can be diverted to your muscles in case you have to "run." This is known as the "fight or flight" response.

The problem with stress hormones in the 21st century is that the fight or flight response isn't usually necessary, because most of our stress is emotional. Occasionally, we may want to flee from a bank robbery or mugger, but most of us just want to flee from our jobs or our kids! In other words, our stress hormones actually put a physical strain on our bodies, and can lower our resistance to disease, which can impact our body from head to toe. We can suffer from stress-related:

- Headaches.
- Gastrointestinal problems.
- Bladder problems.
- Heart problems.
- Back pain.
- High blood pressure.
- High cholesterol.

Good Stress

Good things come from good stress, even though it feels "stressful" or bad in the short term. Stress challenges us to stretch ourselves beyond our capabilities, which is what makes us meet deadlines, push the "outside of the envelope," and invent creative solutions to our problems. Examples of good stress include challenging projects; positive life-changing events (moving, changing jobs, or ending unhealthy relationships); and confronting fears, illness, or people who make us feel bad (this is one of those bad in the short term/good in the long-term situations). Essentially, whenever a stressful event triggers emotional, intellectual, or spiritual growth, it is a "good stress." It is often not the event as much as it is your *response* to the event that determines whether it is a "good" or "bad" stress. The death of a loved one can sometimes lead to personal growth because we may see something about ourselves we did not see before—new resilience, for example. So even a death can be a "good stress," though we grieve and are sad in the short term.

Bad Stress

Bad stress results from boredom and stagnation. When no growth occurs from the stressful event, it is "bad stress." When negative events don't seem to yield anything positive in the long term, but more of the *same*, the stress can lead to chronic and debilitating health problems. This is not to say that we can't get sick from good stress, either, but when there is nothing positive from the stress it has a much more negative effect on our health. Some examples of bad stress include stagnant jobs or relationships, disability from terrible accidents or diseases, or long-term unemployment. These kinds of situations can lead to depression, low self-esteem, and a host of physical illnesses.

Managing stress

For more information on stress management, consult my book, *50 Ways to Prevent and Manage Stress* (McGraw-Hill, 2001) or *Women Managing Stress* (Penguin Books, 2002).

Signs of a Woman's Heart Attack

For women, the symptoms of heart disease, and even an actual heart attack, can be much more vague—seemingly unrelated to heart problems. Signs of heart disease in women include some surprising symptoms, some of which may be masked by thyroid problems. On the other hand, a woman experiencing some of these symptoms may be worried she is having a heart attack, when in fact it is purely thyroid-related. So, please, review this list of symptoms carefully:

➤ Shortness of breath and/or fatigue.

➤ Jaw pain (often masked by arthritis and joint pain).

➤ Pain in the back of the neck (often masked by arthritis or joint pain).

➤ Pain down the right or left arm.

➤ Back pain (often masked by arthritis and joint pain).

➤ Sweating. (Ladies, have your thyroid checked. This is a classic sign of an overactive thyroid gland. Also if you're diabetic, test your blood sugar—you may be low.)

➤ Fainting.

- ➤ Palpitations (Ladies, again—have your thyroid checked, as these are also a classic symptom of an overactive thyroid).

- ➤ Bloating (after menopause, this is a sign of coronary artery blockage).

- ➤ Heartburn, belching, or other gastrointestinal pain (often a sign of an actual heart attack in women).

- ➤ Chest "heaviness" between the breasts. (This is how women experience "chest pain." Some describe it as a "sinking feeling" or burning sensation. Also described as an aching, throbbing, or a squeezing sensation, hot poker tab between the chest, or feeling your heart jump into your throat.)

- ➤ Sudden swings in blood sugar.

- ➤ Vomiting.

- ➤ Confusion.

Clearly, there are plenty of other causes for the symptoms on this list, but it's important that your doctor includes heart disease as a possible cause, rather than dismissing it because your symptoms are not "male," which your doctor may refer to as "typical."

Diagnostic tests that can confirm heart disease in women include a manual exam (doctor examining you with a stethoscope), an electrocardiogram, an exercise stress test, an echocardiogram, and as well as a myriad of imaging tests that may use radioactive substances to take pictures of the heart.

Preventing or Reversing Heart Disease

If you're diagnosed with heart disease, the "cure" is prevention or reversal through diet (see What to Eat), exercise (see How To Move), and protection through hormone replacement therapy, cholesterol-lowering drugs, and possibly blood pressure-lowering drugs. In fact, it's estimated that roughly

90 percent of all heart disease is preventable with lifestyle changes.

Lifestyle changes

By incorporating some of the information in the following two sections, the necessary "lifestyle changes" you need to make, in addition to quitting smoking if you're a smoker and making an attempt to reduce some of your stress (see blood pressure section), you can move toward a healthier life.

What to Eat

The way to a *woman's* heart is through the stomach, too. The most dramatic prevention of heart disease starts with a heart-smart, low-fat diet.

Understanding Fat

Fat is technically known as *fatty acids*, which are crucial nutrients for our cells. We cannot live without fatty acids, or fat. If you looked at each fat molecule carefully, you'd find three different kinds of fatty acids on it: saturated (solid), monounsaturated (less solid, with the exception of olive and peanut oils), and polyunsaturated (liquid) fatty acids. When you see the term "unsaturated fat," it refers to either monounsaturated or polyunsaturated fats.

These three fatty acids combine with glycerol to make what's chemically known as triglycerides. Each fat molecule is a linked chain made up of glycerol, carbon atoms, and hydrogen atoms. The more hydrogen atoms that are on that chain, the more saturated or solid the fat. The liver breaks down fat molecules by secreting bile (stored in the gallbladder)—one of the liver's main functions. The liver also makes cholesterol. Too much saturated fat may cause your liver to overproduce cholesterol, while the triglycerides in your bloodstream will rise, perpetuating the problem.

Fat is therefore a good thing—in moderation. But as with all good things, most of us want too much of it. Excess dietary fat is by far the most damaging element in the Western diet. A gram of fat contains twice the calories as the same amount of protein or carbohydrate. Decreasing the fat in your diet and replacing it with more grain products, vegetables, and fruit is the best way to lower your risk of colon cancer and cardiovascular diseases. Fat in the diet comes from meats, dairy products, and vegetable oils. Other sources of fat include coconuts (60 percent fat), peanuts (78 percent fat), and avocados (82 percent fat). There are different kinds of fatty acids in these sources of fats: saturated, monounsaturated, and polyunsaturated (which, again, is what is meant by the term *unsaturated fat*). And then there is a fourth kind of fat in our diets: transfatty acids. This is a factory-made fat that is found in margarine, for example.

To cut through all this big, fat jargon, you can boil down fat into two categories: "harmful fats" and "helpful fats" (which the popular press often defines as "good fats/bad fats").

Harmful Fats

The following are harmful fats because they can increase your risk of cardiovascular problems, as well as many cancers, including colon and breast cancers. These are fats that are fine in moderation, but harmful in excess (and harmless if not eaten at all):

➤ **Saturated fats.** These are solid at room temperature and stimulate cholesterol production in your body. In fact, the way that saturated fat looks prior to ingesting it is the way it will look when it lines your arteries. Foods high in saturated fat include processed meat, fatty meat, lard, butter, margarine, solid vegetable shortening, chocolate, and tropical oils (coconut oil is more than 90 percent saturated). Saturated fat should be consumed only in very low amounts.

➤ **Transfatty acids.** These are factory-made fats that behave that same way saturated fat does in your body.

Helpful fats

The following are fats that are beneficial to your health and actually protect against certain health problems, including heart disease. These are fats that you are encouraged to use more, rather than less frequently in your diet. In fact, nutritionists suggest that you substitute harmful fats with these:

➢ **Unsaturated fat.** This is partially solid or liquid at room temperature. The more liquid the fat, the more polyunsaturated it is, which, in fact, *lowers* your cholesterol levels. This group of fats includes monounsaturated fats and polyunsaturated fats. Sources of unsaturated fats include vegetable oils (canola, safflower, sunflower, corn) and seeds and nuts. Unsaturated fats come from plants, with the exception of tropical oils, such as coconut.

➢ **Fish fats** (a.k.a. Omega-3 Oils). The fats naturally present in fish that swim in cold waters, known as omega-3 fatty acids or fish oils, arc all polyunsaturated. Again, polyunsaturated fats are good for you: they lower cholesterol levels, are crucial for brain tissue, and protect against heart disease. Look for cold water fish such as mackerel, albacore tuna, salmon, and sardines.

Factory-made fats

An assortment of factory-made fats have been introduced into our diet, courtesy of food producers who are trying to give us the taste of fat without all the calories of saturated fats. Unfortunately, man-made fats offer their own bag of horrors. That's because when a fat is made in a factory, it becomes a "transfatty acid," a harmful fat that *not only* raises the level of "bad" cholesterol (LDL, short for low-density lipids) in your bloodstream, but lowers the amount of "good" cholesterol (HDL, short for high-density lipids) that's already there.

How does a "transfatty acid" come into being? Transfatty acids are what you get when a liquid oil, such as corn oil, is made into a more solid or spreadable substance, such as margarine. Transfatty acids, you might say, are the "road to hell, paved with good intentions." Someone, way back when, thought that if you could take the "good fat"—unsaturated fat—and solidify it, so it could double as butter or lard, you could eat the same things without missing the spreadable fat. That sounds like a great idea. Unfortunately, to make an unsaturated liquid fat more solid, you have to add hydrogen to its molecules. This is known as *hydrogenation*, the process that converts liquid fat to semi-solid fat. That ever-popular chocolate bar ingredient, "hydrogenated palm oil" is a classic example of a trans-fatty acid. Hydrogenation also prolongs the shelf life of a fat, such as polyunsaturated fats, which can oxidize when exposed to air, causing rancid odors or flavors. Deep-frying oils used in the restaurant trade are generally hydrogenated.

What's wrong with transfatty acid?

Trans-fatty acid is sold as a polyunsaturated or monounsaturated fat with a line of advertising copy such as: "made from polyunsaturated vegetable oil." Except in your body, it is treated as a *saturated* fat. So really, transfatty acids are a saturated fat in disguise. The advertiser may, in fact, say that the product contains "no saturated fat" or is "healthier" than the comparable animal or tropical oil product with saturated fat. So be careful out there: *Read your labels.* The magic word you're looking for is *hydrogenated*. If the product lists a variety of unsaturated fats (monounsaturated X oil, polyunsaturated Y oil, and so on), keep reading. If the word *hydrogenated* appears, count that product as a saturated fat; your body will!

Margarine versus butter

There's an old tongue twister: "Betty Botter bought some butter that made the batter bitter; so Betty Botter bought more butter that made the batter better." Are we making our batters bitter or better with margarine? It depends.

Because the news of transfatty acids broke in the late 1980s, margarine manufacturers began to offer some less "bitter" margarines; some contain no hydrogenated oils, and others much smaller amounts. Margarines with less than 60 percent to 80 percent oil (9 to 11 grams of fat) will contain 1.0 to 3.0 grams of trans-fatty acids per serving, compared to butter, which is 53 percent saturated fat. You might say it's a choice between a bad fat and a *worse* fat.

It's also possible for a liquid vegetable oil to retain a high concentration of unsaturated fat when it's been partially hydrogenated. In this case, your body will metabolize this as some saturated fat and some unsaturated fat.

Cut Down on Carbs

Fat is not the only thing that can make you fat: *What about carbohydrates?* You see, a diet high in carbohydrates can also make you fat. That's because carbohydrates—meaning starchy stuff, such as rice, pasta, breads, or potatoes—can be stored as fat when eaten in excess.

Carbohydrates can be simple or complex. Simple carbohydrates are found in any food that has natural sugar (honey, fruits, juices, vegetables, milk) and anything that contains table sugar.

Complex carbohydrates are more sophisticated foods that are made up of larger molecules, such as grain foods, starches, and foods high in fiber.

Normally, all carbs convert into glucose when you eat them. Glucose is the technical term for "simplest sugar." All your energy comes from glucose in your blood—also known as blood glucose or blood sugar—your body fuel. When your blood sugar is used up, you feel weak and tired...and hungry. But what happens when you eat more carbohydrates than your body can use? Your body will store those extra carbs as fat. What we also know is that the rate at which glucose is absorbed by your body from carbohydrates is affected by other parts of your meal, such as the protein, fiber, and fat. If you're eating only carbohydrates and no protein or fat, for example, they will convert into glucose more quickly—to the point where you may feel mood swings, as your blood sugar rises and dips.

Nutrition experts now advise that you seek out a balance of roughly 40 percent of calories of carbs, 30 percent of calories from protein, and 30 percent of calories from unsaturated fats.

Understanding Sugar

Sugars are found naturally in many foods you eat. The simplest form of sugar is glucose, which is what "blood sugar," also called "blood glucose" is—your basic body fuel. You can buy pure glucose at any drugstore in the form of dextrose tablets. Dextrose is just "edible glucose." For example, when you see people having "sugar water" fed to them intravenously, dextrose is the sugar in that water. When you see "dextrose" on a candy-bar label, it means that the candy-bar manufacturer used "edible glucose" in the recipe.

Glucose is the baseline ingredient of all naturally-occurring sugars, which include:

- ➤ Sucrose: table or white sugar, naturally found in sugar cane and sugar beets.
- ➤ Fructose: the natural sugar in fruits and vegetables.
- ➤ Lactose: the natural sugar in all milk products.
- ➤ Maltose: the natural sugar in grains (flours and cereals).

When you ingest a natural sugar of any kind, you're actually ingesting one part glucose and one or two parts of *another* naturally occurring sugar. For example, sucrose is biochemically constructed from one part glucose and one part fructose. So...from glucose it came, and unto glucose it shall return—once it hits your digestive system. The same is true for all naturally occurring sugars, with the exception of lactose. As it happens, lactose breaks down into glucose and an "odd duck" simple sugar, galactose (which I used to think was something in our solar system until I became a health writer). Just think of lactose as the "milky way" and you'll probably remember.

Simple sugars can get a pretty complicated when you discuss their molecular structures. For example, simple sugars can be classified as monosaccharides (a.k.a. "single sugars") or dissaccharides (a.k.a. double sugars). But unless you're writing a chemistry exam on sugars, you don't need to know this confusing stuff. You just need to know that all naturally-occurring sugars wind up as glucose once you eat them; glucose is carried to your cells through the bloodstream and is used as body fuel or energy.

How long does it take for one of the previously mentioned sugars to return to glucose? Well, it greatly depends on the amount of fiber in your food, how much protein you've eaten, and how much fat accompanies the sugar in your meal. If you have enough energy or fuel, once that sugar becomes glucose, it can be stored as fat. And that's how—and why—sugar can make you fat.

Factory-added sugars

What you have to watch out for is *added sugar*; these are sugars that manufacturers add to foods during processing or packaging. Foods containing fruit juice concentrates, invert sugar, regular corn syrup, honey or molasses, hydrolyzed lactose syrup, or high-fructose corn syrup all have added sugars. Many people don't realize, however, that pure, *unsweetened* fruit juice is still a potent source of sugar, even when it contains no added sugar. Extra lactose (naturally occurring sugar in milk products), dextrose ("edible glucose"), and maltose (naturally occurring sugar in grains) are also contained in many of your foods. In other words, the products may have naturally occurring sugars anyway, and then *more* sugar is thrown in to enhance consistency, taste, and so on. The best way to know how much sugar is in a product is to look at the nutritional label for "carbohydrates."

Soluble Fiber

Fiber is the part of a plant your body can't digest, which comes in the form of both water soluble fiber, which *dissolves in* water, and water insoluble fiber, which *absorbs* water; this is what's meant by "soluble" and "insoluble" fiber.

Soluble and insoluble fiber do differ, but they are equally good things. Soluble fiber—somehow—lowers the "bad" LDL in your body. Experts aren't entirely sure how soluble fiber works its magic, but one popular theory is that it gets mixed into the bile the liver secretes, and forms a gel that traps the building blocks of cholesterol, thus lowering your LDL levels. It's akin to a spiderweb trapping smaller insects. Sources of soluble fiber include oats or oat bran, legumes, some seeds, carrots, oranges, and bananas. Soybeans are also high sources of soluble fiber. Studies show that people with very high cholesterol have the most to gain by eating soybeans. Soybean is also a *phytoestrogen* (plant estrogen) that is believed to lower the risks of estrogen-related cancers (for example, breast cancer), as well as lower the incidence of estrogen-loss symptoms associated with menopause.

Insoluble fiber doesn't affect your cholesterol levels at all, but it regulates your bowel movements. This is discussed in Chapter 4.

Whole-grain breads are good sources of insoluble fiber (flax bread is particularly good because flaxseeds are a source of soluble fiber, too). The problem is understanding what is truly "whole grain." For example, there is an assumption that because bread is dark or brown, it's more nutritious; this *is not* so. In fact, many brown breads are simply enriched white breads dyed with molasses. ("Enriched" means that nutrients lost during processing have been replaced.) High-fiber pita breads and bagels are available, but you have to search for them. A good rule is to simply look for the phrase "whole wheat." This wheat is, indeed, whole.

Alcohol

Alcohol delivers about seven calories per gram or 150 calories per drink. It's the sugar *in* that alcoholic beverage that can also pack in more calories. That said, alcohol has been shown in studies to raise your "good" cholesterol (HDL), when the so-called "French Paradox" was investigated, and red wine was believed to have heart-healthy benefits.

Fine wine

Dry wines that are listed as (0), meaning no added sugar or "dry," means it has calories but no sugar. The same thing goes for cognac, brandy, and dry sherry that contain no sugar.

Wine is the result of natural sugar in fruits or fermenting fruit juices. Fermentation means that natural sugar is converted into alcohol. On the other hand, a sweet wine listed as (3) means that it contains three grams of sugar per 100 mL or 3.5-oz portion. Dessert wines or ice wines are really sweet; they contain about 15 percent sugar or 10 grams of sugar for a two-oz serving. Sweet liqueurs are 35 percent sugar.

A glass of dry wine with your meal adds about 100 calories. Half soda water and half wine (a spritzer) contains half the calories. When you cook with wine, the alcohol evaporates, leaving only the flavor.

At the pub

If you're a beer drinker, you're basically having some corn, barley, and a couple of teaspoons of malt sugar (maltose) when you have a bottle of beer. The corn and barley ferment into mostly alcohol and some maltose. That's about 150 calories per bottle, plus 3 tsp of malt sugar. A light beer has fewer calories but contains at least 100 calories per bottle.

The hard stuff

The stiffer the drink, the fatter it gets. Hard liquors such as scotch, rye, gin, and rum are made out of cereal grains; vodka, the Russian staple, is made out of potatoes. In this case, the grains ferment into alcohol. Hard liquor averages about 40-percent alcohol but has no sugar. Nevertheless, you're looking at about 100 calories per small shot glass, so long as you don't add fruit juice, tomato juice, or sugary soft drinks.

Herbs for the Heart

Herbs that are good for the uterus are also good for the heart. Plants that strengthen the uterus and the heart are either green or red, such as hawthorn, strawberry, raspberry, and motherwort. As a general rule, if you're experiencing hot flashes or night sweats, this can trigger heart palpitations. Drinking lots of water, mineral-rich herbal infusions, fresh grape juice or grapes will help you retain fluids and reduce palpitations.

To nourish/tone the heart

> Wheat germ oil. One or more tablespoons/15 ml daily.

> Vitamin E oil. One or more tablespoons daily.

> Flaxseed (*Linum usitatissimum*), also known as linseed is considered the best heart oil—but only if it is absolutely fresh and taken uncooked. One

to 3 tsp/5–15 ml of flaxseed oil first thing in the morning is recommended. You can also grind the seeds and sprinkle them on cereals or salads. You can also soak flaxseeds in water and drink the whole thing first thing in the morning.

➣ Other heart-protective oils can be found in the fresh pressed oils of borage seed, or black currant seed.

➣ Other essential fatty acids can be found in plantain, lamb's quarter, or amaranth.

➣ Hawthorn berry tincture. Twenty-five–40 drops of the berry tincture up to four times a day. Expect results no sooner than six to eight weeks.

➣ Seaweed.

➣ Carotene-rich foods. Look for bright colored fruits and vegetables. The richer the color, the richer they are in carotene.

➣ Garlic, Knoblauch *(Allium sativum)*. Greatest heart benefits come from eating it raw, but you can also purchase deodorized caplets.

➣ Lemon balm. Steep a handful of fresh leaves in a glass of white wine for an hour or so and drink it with dinner. Or make lemon balm vinegar to use on your salads.

➣ Dandelion root tincture. Use 10–15 drops with meals.

➣ Ginseng *(Panax quinquefolium)*. Chew on the root or use five to 40 drops of tincture.

➣ Motherwort *(Leonurus cardiaca)*. Use a tincture of the flowering tops, five to 15 drops several times a day as needed.

To calm the heart

- Rose flower essence.

- Hawthorn (Crataegus). Try 25–40 drops up to four times a day. Slow-acting, it requires about a month of use before you see results.

- Motherwort tincture. Ten to 20 drops with meals and before bed or 25 to 50 drops for immediate relief.

- Valerian root. As a tea or tincture.

- Ginger root tea, hot or cold. (May aggravate hot flashes and heavy flows.)

- A piece of real licorice root to slow palpitations.

Blood thinning herbs

Blood thinners, such as aspirin, can reduce the incidence of a stroke or heart attack. A daily spoonful of vinegar made from the leaves, buds, and/or flowers of any of the following herbs can give you the same health benefits of aspirin, but also help calcium absorption and improve your digestion. Do not take blood-thinning herbs if you are bleeding heavily, or require surgery.

Alfalfa.

Birch.

Sweet clover.

Bedstraws.

Poplar.

Red clover.

Willow.

Wintergreen.

Black haw (Viburnum). As a tincture, try a 25-drop dose as needed.

Supplements

> **Niacin.** Recommended dose is 500 mg with meals (three times a day). This can initially cause a hot flash-like flush for about 30 minutes after you ingest it. The more regularly you take it, the less often you will flush, if at all. Discontinue if you feel nauseated or have any gastrointestinal distress

> **Magnesium.** Slows palpitations. Check with your doctor about appropriate dosages.

To Lower Blood Pressure

➤ **Hawthorn.** As a tincture, 10 to 20 drops three times daily

➤ **Motherwort.** As a tincture, 10 to 20 drops three times daily.

➤ **Dandelion root.** As a tincture, Use 10 to 15 drops with meals.

➤ **Potassium.** Eighty to 85 percent of people who eat six portions of potassium rich foods daily will reduce their need for blood pressure lowering medication by half or more.

➤ **Raw garlic.** Just 1/2 to one clove of raw garlic a day can dramatically reduce your blood pressure. Mince it and add to eggs, rice, or potatoes.

➤ **Ginseng.**

➤ **Seaweed.**

How to Move

If you look up the word *aerobic* in the dictionary, what you'll find is the chemistry definition: "living in free oxygen." This is certainly correct; we are all aerobes—beings that require oxygen to live. Some bacteria, for example, are anaerobic; they can exist in an environment without oxygen. All that jumping around and fast movement are done to create faster breathing, so we can take in more oxygen into our bodies.

Why are we doing this? Because the blood contains *oxygen*! The faster your blood flows, the more oxygen can flow to your organs. But when your healthcare practitioner tells you to "exercise" or to take up "aerobic exercise," he or she is not referring solely to "increasing oxygen" but to exercising the heart muscle. The faster it beats, the better "workout" it gets (although you don't want to *over*work your heart, either).

An exercise is considered aerobic if it makes your heart beat faster than it does at rest. When your heart is beating fast, you'll be breathing hard and sweating and will officially be in your "target zone" or "ideal range" (the kind of phrases that turn many people off).

There are official calculations you can do to find this target range. For example, it's recommended that by subtracting your age from 220, then multiplying that number by 60 percent, you will find your "threshold level"—which means your heart should be beating X beats per minute for 20 to 30 minutes. If you multiply the number by 75 percent, you will find your "ceiling level"—which means your heart should not be beating faster than X beats per minute for 20 to 30 minutes. But this is only an example. If you are on heart medications, you'll want to make sure you discuss what "target" to aim for with your health professional.

Improving Oxygen Flow

When more oxygen is in our bodies, we burn fat, our breathing improves, our blood pressure improves, and our hearts work better—which benefits our entire body, leading to regularity, for example. Oxygen also lowers triglycerides and cholesterol, increasing our high HDL, while decreasing our LDL. This means that your arteries will unclog and you may significantly decrease your risk of heart disease and stroke. More oxygen makes our brains work better, so we feel better. Studies show that depression is decreased when we increase oxygen flow into our bodies. Ancient techniques such as yoga, which specifically improve mental and spiritual well-being, achieve this by combining deep breathing and stretching, which improves oxygen and blood flow to specific parts of the body.

Exercise has been shown to dramatically decrease the incidence of many other diseases, including cancer. Some research suggests that cancer cells tend to thrive in an oxygen-depleted environment. The more oxygen in the bloodstream, the less suseptable you make your body to cancer. In addition, because many cancers are related to fat-soluble toxins, the less fat on your body, the less fat-soluble toxins your body can accumulate.

The only kind of exercise that will burn fat is aerobic exercise because *oxygen burns fat*. If you were to go to your fridge and pull out some animal fat (chicken skin, red-meat fat, or butter), throw it in the sink and light it with a match, it will burn. What makes the flame yellow is oxygen; what fuels the fire is the fat. That same process goes on in your body. The oxygen will burn your fat, however, you increase the oxygen flow in your body through jumping around/increasing heart rate or employing an established deep-breathing technique.

You can increase the flow of oxygen into your bloodstream without exercising your heart muscle by learning how to breathe deeply through your diaphragm. There are many yogic programs and videos available that can teach you this technique, which does not require you to jump around. The benefit is that you would be increasing the oxygen flow into your bloodstream, which is better than doing nothing at all to improve your health, and has many health benefits, according to a myriad of wellness practitioners. Deep-breathing exercises can also help to strengthen digestion and keep you regular.

Finding your pulse

You have pulse points all over your body. The easiest ones to find are those on your neck, at the base of your thumb, just below your earlobe, or on your wrist. To check your heart rate, look at a watch or clock and begin to count your beats for 15 seconds (if the second hand is on the 12, count until it reaches the 3). Then multiply the number of beats by four to get your pulse.

The Borg's Rate of Perceived Exertion

The Borg's Rate of Perceived Exertion (RPE) is a way of measuring exercise intensity without finding your pulse and because of its simplicity, is now the recommended method for judging exertion. This Borg "scale" (as it's dubbed) goes from 6-20. Extremely light activity may rate 7, for example, whereas a very hard activity may rate 19. Exercise practitioners recommend that you do a "talk test" to rate your exertion, too. If you can't talk without gasping for air, you may be working too hard. You should be able to carry on a normal conversation throughout your activity. RPE is extremely individual; what one person rates a 7 another may rate a 10.

Suggested Activities

MORE INTENSE	LESS INTENSE
Skiing	Golf
Running	Bowling
Jogging	Badminton
Stair-Stepping or Stair-Climbing	Crocket
Trampoling	Sailing
Jumping Rope	Swimming

Fitness Walking

Race Walking

Aerobic Classes

Roller Skating

Ice-Skating

Biking

Weight-Bearing Exercises

Tennis

Swimming

Strolling

Stretching

Note: Certain activities, such as wrestling or weightlifting, are usually short but very intense. As a result, people with certain health problems may not be able to partake. For example, if you have heart problems, have diabetes, or are taking medications that can affect your heart, intense exercise is not recommended.

Variations on Jogging

➤ After warming up with a 15-minute walk, simply walk quickly with maximum exertion for two minutes, then slow down for one minute. Keep your heart rate up on the downhill portion of a walk or a hike by adding lunges or squats.

➤ Vary the way you walk for coordination and balance. Try lifting the knees as high as you can, as if marching. Alternate with a shuffle, letting the tips of your fingers touch the ground as you walk. Do a sideways "crab" walk. To strengthen the rarely used muscles of the ankles and feet, walk first on the outsides, then on the insides of your feet, or practice walking backwards.

➤ Use a curb for a step workout, or climb stairs two at a time.

Water Workouts

➤ Start by walking in water that's relatively shallow (waist- or chest-deep). Your breathing and heartbeat will determine how hard you are working. Because you'll be moving fairly slowly, pay attention to your body.

➤ For all-over leg toning, take 50 steps forward, 50 steps sideways fashion, 50 steps backward, then 50 steps to the other side.

➤ To tone your arms, submerge yourself from the neck down, bringing the arms in and out as if clapping. The water will provide natural resistance.

➤ Deep-water workouts are the most difficult, because every move you make is met with resistance. Wear a flotation vest and run without touching the bottom for optimum exertion and little to no impact.

➤ You may also want to try buoyant ankle cuffs and styrofoam dumbells or kickboards for full-body conditioning in the water.

Deep Breathing

➤ Deep relaxation and yoga breathing, such as alternate nostril breath, calms the sympathetic nervous system, thus relaxing the small arteries and permanently lowering blood pressure.

Breast Health

Let's not beat around the bush: the term *breast health* really means, *what can I do to avoid breast cancer?* That's what this chapter is about: all the latest information on mammography, genetic screening, and detection and prevention of breast cancer, including information on tamoxifen as a prevention drug. This chapter *does not* explore breast cancer treatment, which is thoroughly covered in my book *The Breast Sourcebook, Second edition* (McGraw-Hill, 1999).

Reviewing the Known Risk Factors

Seventy percent of women who develop breast cancer have no known risk factors. Given that statistic, what does it mean when you are told you're at risk for breast cancer—or any other disease? A few things, depending on the adjective that *precedes* the word risk. As previously discussed, the risks you can do something about are considered modifiable risk factors. These are risks that can be reduced, prevented, or altered through *behavior* (such as quitting smoking or dieting). The risks you can't do anything about, such as your age or family history, can still be lowered by eliminating modifiable risk factors. The following "risk list" is arranged alphabetically to make it easier for you to access the information you may want *right now*!

Age

The risk of breast cancer is largely age-related because it's rare to see breast cancer under 30, less common to see it between the ages of 30 and 40, and most common in developed nations after menopause (or after 50). For example, looking at North American statistics from 1984 to 1988, only 0.9 per 100,000 women were diagnosed with breast cancer in the 20–24 age group compared to 66.2 per 100,000 cases of breast cancer in the 30–34 age group. However, in women 45–49 years of age, that number rose to 187.4 per 100,000 women, increased to 220 per 100,000 in the 50–54 age group, leaped up to 390.7 per 100,000 women in the 65-69 age group, and peaked at 461.4 per 100,000 women in the 75-79 age group. So, the "one in eight" figure refers to your risk over a lifetime, assuming that you live to be 95 years old.

Another way of looking at your age-related risk is to break it down into five-year increments (assuming American statistics). In this case, by age 30, you have a one in 2,525 chance of developing breast cancer; by age 35, it jumps to one in 622; by age 40, the figure rises to one in 217; by 45, it's one in 93; by 50, one in 50, by 55, it's one in 33; by 60 it's one in 24; by 65, one in 17, by 70, one in 14; by 75, one in 11; by 80, one in 10; by 85, one in 9; and older is one in 8.

Bad Habits

Any lifestyle indulgence that has proven risk factors is considered a "bad habit." If you smoke, drink an excessive amount of alcohol, or abuse illegal drugs, your risk of getting some diseases is higher than people who don't do these things.

Alcohol and cigarettes have been linked to a variety of cancers; breast cancer is no exception. A 1994 survey conducted by the American Cancer Society suggested that smokers were 25 percent more likely than nonsmokers or ex-smokers to die of breast cancer. This is different than saying that smoking causes breast cancer, however. It say "nonsmokers have a better chance of avoiding breast cancer than smokers." It might also mean that smokers who get breast cancer are more likely to die of it. However, smoking does *conclusively* cause lung cancer, currently the number-one cancer killer of women.

As for alcohol, a 1993 National Institutes of Health (NIH) study found that two alcoholic drinks per day could raise your estrogen levels enough to increase your risk of breast-cancer by 40 to 100 percent over women who do not drink at all. In this study, 34 women had their blood levels checked mid-cycle and were found to have a 31.9 percent increase in estrogen over women who were not drinking. Of course, it's also been shown that one to two glasses of wine per day for men and one to three alcoholic beverages *per week* for women may lower the risk of heart disease. The alcohol raises your HDL, thus reducing the deposits of cholesterol in the arterial walls.

As for illegal drugs, such as cocaine, your risks of suffering a drug-related overdose or other health problems should be your main concern.

Bras

In his book, *Dressed to Kill: The Link Between Breast Cancer and Bras*, medical anthropologist Sydney Ross Singer raises the question of whether bras cause breast cancer. He compared women in five U.S. cities who wore bras to those who didn't and concluded that women who wore bras had a higher breast cancer risk. Based on interviews with 4,700 women, Singer and his co-author wife claim that bras constrict the lymph system thus preventing it from "draining and flushing out toxins." The buildup of toxins in breast tissue, according to Singer, triggers lumps, bumps, and cancer. Doctors say this is pure nonsense and point out that, if this were true, then most breast cancers would not occur in the outer upper quadrant of the breasts where the bras restrict the *least*! According to Singer, wearing a bra 24 hours a day increases a woman's risk 125-fold, but removing it for two weeks "cures" *fibrocystic breast condition* (which, by the way, does not mean breast cancer). According to doctors, Singer's hypothesis is a complete fallacy because there are many women who do not wear bras who still have fibrocystic breast condition! Doctors call Singer's study either "bad science" or "junk science" because he has not factored out the influence of other significant breast cancer risk factors, such as diet, for example. One doctor wrote to me that "[Singer's] study is just awful. You could use his methods to prove anything you want."

What Singer may have stumbled across is the issue of the breast being held too close to body temperature. Males with undecended testicles, for example, have a higher incidence of testicular cancer. It's also been noted in some medical texts that girls who wear tight bras can develop hyperprolactinemia (a condition where there's too much prolactin in your system).

Singer also raises the notion that braless cultures seen in Africa or Asia have low rates of breast cancer, whereas African- and Asian-American women, who do wear bras, have high rates of breast cancer. However, keep in mind that the diet in these cultures are lower in fat and often high in fish and sea vegetables, the women have more children, have their first children *earlier*, and breastfeed longer. In addition, North America is more industrialized, and, where there's industry, there are higher rates of breast cancer. This could be due to some cultural differences such as fewer children, later first children, less breastfeeding, and higher longevity rates. So don't burn your bra again just yet, but you can certainly go braless if you like. Massaging your breasts daily apparently helps get the blood flowing properly.

In fact, some theories hold that nipple stimulation may reduce breast cancer risk by clearing free radicals and/or raising oxytocin and lowering prolactin (hormones that control milk production).

Demographics

Who gets breast cancer largely depends on where people live. Industrialized countries have much higher breast cancer rates than underdeveloped countries. Region dramatically affects the rates of breast cancer, and we just don't know why. For instance, the breast cancer rate in Geneva is double that of Spain—even though they are not that far apart geographically. In San Francisco, the rate is double that of Newfoundland's, proving that breast cancer, in North America, can vary from coast to coast.

More interesting, a 1992 *New England Journal of Medicine* article concluded that people migrating from regions with low rates of breast cancer increased their own risk when they entered a country with higher incidences of breast cancer. This proves that breast cancer is largely due to environmental factors, such as lifestyle, culture, diet, water, and air quality.

The risk of breast cancer in North America is also about 30 percent higher in urban communities than rural ones and, as a result, is higher in black communities than white.

The bottom line is that where there's heavy industry, there are higher cancer rates of all kinds. In the United States, the northeastern states comprise the five highest cancer death rates in the United States; the rural western and southern states comprise the five lowest cancer death rates. In Canada, British Columbia, Ontario, and Quebec have higher cancer rates than other parts of Canada. In Europe, the extremes in cancer deaths can be found. England has the highest cancer mortality rates in the world, whereas southern Italy has exceptionally low cancer mortality rates.

Environmental Factors

Environmental factors are extremely important when assessing your risk of breast cancer. Although radiation exposure from modern day X-rays is not a concern, aside from the chemical soup discussed further on pages 91–94, high dose radiation exposure is a concern. For example, if your breasts were exposed to high-dose radiation, this can increase your risk of breast cancer—especially if you were exposed around the time of your first menstrual period. This could mean either direct radiation from a high-dose X-ray, or from radiation emitted during a nuclear explosion or accident.

For the record, women living near areas with high levels of radioactive fallout have higher incidences of a variety of cancers, including breast cancer. We know this because women survivors of Hiroshima and Nagasaki were extensively followed. The breast cancer rates dramatically rose within the entire female population, but particularly increased within younger women in their teens and 20s. The most recent conclusion of this data is that the largest number of breast cancer cases were seen in women who were younger than 10 years of age when they were exposed to fallout. Women who were older when exposed did not seem to be vulnerable to this effect. Breasts may become more resistant to radiation as they mature.

Similar studies have backed up this "early radiation exposure" risk. In North America, women who were checked for tuberculosis (TB) as children with fluoroscopy (high dose X-rays where the picture was taken as the child breathed in) in the 1930s and 40s were found to have higher rates of breast cancer. A Rochester study found that women treated with radiation for mastitis (bacterial breast infection) from the 1920s to the 60s also had higher rates of breast cancer. The same goes for women treated with radiation as children for acne, enlarged thymus glands (primarily in infants), and anyone subjected to the equivalent of one X-ray per week for two years in childhood (as in those with scoliosis, for example).

Some studies have found the increase in risk is directly proportional to the radiation dose. Radiation was also widely used to determine fetal positions in prenatal care (during the 30s and 40s, known as pelvimetry, which exposed the *fetal* breast tissue to radiation) and was used to treat asthma, pneumonia, whooping cough, and even hyperthyroidism. Let's not forget the radiation used to treat congenital heart problems, as well as those standard TB exams most employers demanded between 1920 and 1960. Radiation was also widely used by chiropractors to determine spinal column alignment, and by shoe retailers, who used high-dose X-rays on the feet to find out the shoe size.

In his book, *Preventing Breast Cancer: The Story of a Major, Proven, Preventable Cause of This Disease* (1995), John W. Gofman, M.D., Ph.D., concludes that about 3/4 of breast cancer cases are largely due to past medical-related radiation. In other words, women who received radiation as children or young women may be able to link their breast cancers to that period in their life. He also suggests that much of the radiation therapy between the 1920s and 60s was probably poorly documented (that is, much more was done than we think). Gofman states that 75 percent of the women who have recently had breast cancer or are currently diagnosed would probably never have developed it if medicine had never used irradiation. Gofman also states that there is no safe level of radiation; even low-dose radiation can cause cancer (but at much lower rates than high-dose radiation).

Electromagnetic fields

Researchers are still trying to see if electromagnetic fields (that is areas near power lines) can predispose people who live near them or people who work under them to higher rates of cancer. Some studies have found the increase in breast cancer risk is directly proportional to the radiation dose.

Environmental estrogens

The role of chemical pollutants seems to be far more ominous than any single environmental factor. In 1994, a major discovery led many medical researchers and environmental scientists to the same conclusion: Life on planet Earth is being threatened by a group of substances known as "environmental estrogens." A very long grocery list of organic chemicals, found in various pesticides and plastics, is transforming in the natural environment into a substance that is identical to the female hormone, estrogen. And the results are absolutely disastrous, threatening not only human fertility, but contributing to an epidemic of reproductive cancers, such as breast cancer in women and testicular cancer in men. These chemicals are also disrupting several wildlife species, which are now being born as hermaphrodites or sterile. In Florida, for example, the majority of male alligators are sterile as a result of either non-developed or abnormally shaped penises. A chemical spill in nearby waters was found to be the culprit, which was having an "estrogenic effect" on the alligators' natural habitat.

One of the worst organic chemical culprits is nonylphenol, which is used in hundreds of everyday consumer products, such as detergents, toiletries, cosmetics, and oils. It also lines the insides of canned goods; it's found in various plastic food wraps; and it's found in spermicides and contraceptive foam and a variety of other products. The scientific literature is slowly becoming saturated with findings linking one organic chemical after another to reproductive cancers and "endocrine disruption" in both wildlife and humans.

Organic chemicals are in the air we breathe from numerous air pollutants, in the food preservatives used in numerous canned and packaged goods, and in the pesticides used on fresh produce. These chemicals then contaminate the water and soil, which contaminate the entire human food chain. Some suggest that environmental estrogens are "feminizing" the planet. Some suggest women are perhaps being "overloaded" with estrogen, which may be associated with the rise of estrogen-dependent cancers, as well as estrogen-related conditions, such as endometriosis and fibroids. Estrogen pollutants are also thought to accumulate in fatty tissues (estrogen pollutants are fat). Because women generally carry more body fat than men, women may be accumulating more of these toxins. Some studies have already found that women with breast cancer tended to have higher concentrations of the organochlorines (a type of manmade chemical) DDT, DDE, or PCBs in their fat tissue. In fact elevated levels of DDE in the blood have been directly linked to a fourfold increase of breast cancer in the United States. We already know that dioxins, also organocholorines, are associated with endometriosis. Pesticides are major contributors to this environmental estrogen problem, one of the most notorious of which is DDT. DDT stands for "dichloro-diphenyl-trichlore-ethane" and was formally banned in most industrialized countries by the mid-1970s. But even though DDT has been pretty much banned in most countries since 1972, it remains active in the environment for 25 to 30 years.

A case in point

One of the strongest cases to link pesticides such as DDT to breast cancer is the Isreali pesticide ban of the 70s. Faced with one of the highest breast cancer rates in the world by the 70s, the Israeli government decided to ban three pesticides: a-BHC (benzine hexachloride, or hexachlorocyclohexane), y-BHC (lindane), and DDT. Israel's agricultural boom in the 60s and 70s led to far higher concentrations of these pesticides than in countries such as the United States. For example, concentrations of DDE, the DDT byproduct, were about 500 percent higher in Israeli milk than U.S. milk prior to the ban. It was reported that the breast cancer mortality rate was double that of countries with similar fat consumption. So, it was decided that these three pesticides were to be phased out by 1978. Apparently, between 1976 and 1986 Israel's breast cancer rate was reported to have dropped by nearly 8 percent, even though breast cancer rates were rising everywhere else. Factor in the global increase of breast rates at the time, and the statistic you get is a 20-percent drop.

A 1990 paper published in the *Annals of the New York Academy of Science* concluded that the drop in breast cancer rates in Israel was directly linked to the country's ban on pesticides.

Isreali statistics criticized

Not everyone buys the Isreali breast cancer story, however. Many critics point out that there were simply too many other factors *not* taken into consideration. For example, between 1976 and 1986, were more women having children? Were more women having children earlier? Was there an increase in breastfeeding? And what about immigration from other countries with lower breast cancer rates?

Dr. Bruce Dunn from British Columbia argues that the study that reported the drop in breast cancer rates was flawed, in that it did not account for year-to-year natural fluctuations in cancer rates.

Dunn argues that, had the study compared breast cancer rates for the years 1975 and 1985 (instead of 1976 and 1986), it would have found a 62 percent increase in breast cancer deaths in young women. And, had it looked at mortality data from 1965 to 1988, the rate of breast cancer in Israel would have been found to remain almost constant.

It's estimated that billions of gallons of these toxic substances have been released onto an unsuspecting environment. Because these chemicals are resistant to breaking down, they're spread around the world through the air and water, exposing us to these poisons in our food, groundwater, surface water, and air. According to a 1992 Greenpeace report on chlorine and human health, no industrial organochlorines are known to be *non*-toxic.

Estrogen

High levels of estrogen seem to be markers for increased risk of breast cancer. But the estrogen question is complicated, because there are times in your life when estrogen levels are high, such as during pregnancy or during certain times in your cycle. Fat cells also make estrogen, but this isn't a concern until *after* menopause. Sources of extra estrogen include:

➢ Exposure to DES (diethylstilbestrol), a drug administered to pregnant women from the 1940s to the 70s to supposedly stop miscarriage. DES daughters are at risk for a variety of reproductive cancers, mainly vaginal and cervical. Breast cancer is more likely if you are a DES daughter, however. For more information, contact the DES Cancer Network at (510)–465–4011.

➢ Hormone Replacement Therapy (see Chapter 1) or birth control pills after age 35.

➢ Dietary fat (see "What To Eat"). This is not an external source of estrogen, but may contribute to your fat cells production of estrogen if the fat you eat, makes you fat!

➢ Hormone-fed produce (see "What To Eat").

➢ Environmental estrogens.

Please keep in mind, though, that estrogen levels are hard to calculate and are often misread by various researchers. The level can vary with the time of day, menstrual cycle, pregnancy, and lactation. Studies that base their conclusions on a single measurement of estrogen in women may result in confusing or contradictory results. The reading will be true for each woman at the *time* it was taken, but the degree to which the reading can be taken as an indicator of that woman's overall estrogen exposure is questionable.

Exercise

As do our diets, exercise also plays a huge role in lowering our risk of a variety of health problems. Breast cancer is one of those. The more we exercise, the more fat we burn, the more oxygen is carried to our muscles, and the better our bodies work. On average, women who do four hours of exercise per week may reduce their risks of premenopausal breast cancer by as much as 58 percent. Women with no children lowered their risks by 27 percent, and women *with* children their risks by as much as 72 percent. But again, exercise is only *associated* with lower breast cancer risk. We don't know what *other* factors are at work. Are both diet and exercise and some other unknown factors associated with breast cancer risk? Are women who are predisposed to breast cancer less inclined to exercise anyway? We just don't know. When exercise is strenuous, that ovarian function is decreased and hence estrogen levels are lower. In athletes, for example, periods may stop altogether (called amennorhea), which does lower breast cancer risk. What we also know is that people who exercise regularly tend to eat better.

The younger you begin regular exercise, the more you may be protected from breast cancer. Even so, women who don't get started until later in life are still more protected than women who are sedentary.

The best forms of exercise, according to a number of studies, are jogging, racquet sports, swimming, strenuous walking and weight-lifting. It's suggested that a range of activities is the best kind of program (probably because it relieves boredom and monotony).

HRT

This is discussed on page 31 in Chapter 1.

Menstrual History

Unfortunately, your menstrual history can apparently affect your risk of breast cancer, but many experts are in conflict as to how significant a role it truly plays in the big picture. For example, one factor is what experts call "early menarche." Menarche refers to your first period; early menarche means that you got your first period prior to age 12. This somewhat trivial detail also means that you've been making estrogen longer than the average woman has, which is why this is even looked at. Menarche levels can vary enormously. The average age of menarche is 12.8 in the United States and 17 in China. Some researchers say this why breast cancer occurrence in China is 1/3 that of the United States. And even within China, provinces with later menarche tend to have lower rates of breast cancer.

Another factor is cycle length. If your cycles are either longer or shorter than average, your breast cancer risk increases by some estimates as high as 50 percent. (An average cycle is anywhere from 26–29 days.) It's believed that shorter or longer cycles indicate a hormonal imbalance at work, which *may* contribute to an increased breast cancer risk. Shorter cycles also indicate that you're making more estrogen than women with longer cycles.

Pregnancy History

This is a *huge* factor in determining your overall risk of breast cancer. In fact, according to a 1751 edition of the *Chambers Encyclopedia,* breast cancer is described as "a most dread disease, particularly of the celibate and barren." To a large extent, this is still true today.

For example, according to the NCI, lesbians are two to three times more likely to develop breast cancer than heterosexual women (because heterosexual women are more likely to bear children), and childfree women are 50 percent more likely to develop breast cancer than women who have borne children under 35. The more pregnancies you have, the lower your risks are. Curiously, if you bear your first child after 35, your pregnancy no longer offers you the same protection against breast cancer—*unless you decide to breastfeed*.

Abortion

Your pregnancy history can be a paradox in terms of breast cancer risk. For example, the more full-term pregnancies a woman has, the lower her risk of developing breast cancer after menopause. But women who've had children may be more likely to get breast cancer before they reach age 35. Also, if the pregnancy was interrupted through a therapeutic abortion (that is, surgical termination of a pregnancy vs. a miscarriage), some studies indicate that the risks of breast cancer may increase. Here's why:

Once you become pregnant, even if it is terminated, your breasts have changed in structure. The hormonal symphony that controls the pregnancy causes cellular changes in your breasts as well as tissue growth. Throughout the pregnancy, the breasts continue to change until they reach their final maturation prior to delivery, when you're physically able to breastfeed. However, if a pregnancy ends in the first trimester, all the changes your breasts have been going through suddenly stop, making the cells less stable and possibly more vulnerable to cancer. Even if subsequent pregnancies go to term, your risks are apparently slightly increased as a result of an abortion. Some studies argue that the more abortions you have, the greater your risk, but this is highly debatable. These studies remain inconclusive.

There is a sharp contrast to women who carry their first baby to term. In this case, these women reduce their risk of breast cancer by roughly 50 percent. Women who abort may be at greater risk if they're 18 or under, they're aborting after eight weeks, or breast cancer runs in their family.

Interestingly, one study found that women who aborted, but later breastfed, did not seem to have an increased risk of breast cancer.

Weight

The more fat in your cultural diet, the higher the rate of breast cancer in your cultural group. This may be due to the fat eaten or may be due to other dietary or lifestyle differences between cultures. However, the more fat on your body, the greater your risk of breast cancer may be as well. That's because fat cells store estrogen and manufacture it, increasing your risk of estrogen-dependent cancers, as well as a number of other diseases.

Apples and pears

Although we can all do something about our weight, it's difficult to do much about our body shapes. But unfortunately, one study has actually linked body shapes to breast cancer. Apparently, pear-shaped figures (where extra weight is carried in the hips and thighs) are less at risk for breast cancer than apple-shaped figures (where extra weight is carried around the waist). Lots of data indicates that the fat in our spare-tire area is more metabolically active than the fat on our thighs, hips, and buttocks. The apple-shape theory was refuted by researchers from the Memorial Sloan-Kettering Cancer Center, who reported in 1993 that they found no such link. Interestingly, smoking changes fat metabolism so that the fat is distributed more in the middle (spare-tire area). This may not increase your risk of breast cancer, because *smoking* is also linked to earlier menopause.

Should You Be Worried?

Because most women grossly overestimate their risk of breast cancer by as many as four times, if you're worried about it, it's probably worth the money to have some peace of mind and a more realistic perspective. Again, if you're looking for answers solely based on "known" risk factors, you probably won't get much more than you would from a tealeaf reading. Because, again, 70 percent of the women who develop breast cancer do *not* have any of the known risk factors. In the meantime, use the following guidelines to help you make your decision about counseling:

You have reason to worry about breast cancer over the age of 50 if:

1. You have a first-degree relative (mother, sister, or daughter) who has/had breast cancer.

2. You have a first-degree relative who has/had colon, ovarian, or endometrial cancer.

3. You had breast, colon, ovarian, or endometrial cancer.

4. Other than mammography and diagnostic chest X-rays, you've been exposed to high dose X-rays or high-dose radiation to your chest area. (again, fluoroscopy or nuclear fallout).

5. You have dense breast tissue (and more problems with interpreting mammogram results).

6. You have had breast biopsies done for benign breast problems, excluding fibroadenomas.

7. You had an early menarche (early period).

8. You did not breastfeed (minor reason).

9. You are obese or eat large amounts of fat (minor reason).

10. You have never been pregnant (minor reason).

11. You are a DES daughter (minor reason).

You MAY have reason to worry about breast cancer under or over the age of 50 if:

1. You have testred positive for a breast cancer gene or have first-degree relatives who developed breast cancer prior to age 50.

2. You have more years of education than average (there are some cultural/lifestyle risks associated with this).

3. You don't eat many fruits or vegetables.

4. You live in a highly industrialized area with many chemical plants nearby.

5. You're exposed to estrogenic chemicals in your work or residence.

Genetic Screening

The fact that some families were predisposed to getting cancer was first recorded by the Romans in A.D. 100. Many cancers run in families, but it's particularly true with breast, ovarian, and colon cancers. That's why research into a specific cancer gene (discussed next) is an important step in identifying women at risk. "First-degree" relatives are the ones that determine whether you have a strong family history of breast cancer. That means that in order to qualify, either your mother or sister (or on rare occasions, daughter) would have been diagnosed with breast cancer. The younger they were at the time of their diagnosis, the more at risk you are. Grandmothers, great aunts, and paternal relatives are not as crucial in determining family histories. However, if breast cancer was diagnosed in your maternal aunt (your mother's sister), there is a stronger likelihood that it runs in the family. Familial breast cancer, however, accounts for only 5 to 10 percent of all breast cancers diagnosed. One study also found that daughters of men with prostate cancer were at a higher risk of developing breast cancer.

What about genes?

Well, since about 1940, researchers have known that cancer is caused by mutating cells. This used to be attributed to simply aging cells in aging bodies, but we now realize that there are genes that *control* mutation, and some genes have more control over mutation than others. There is a phenomenon called *oncogenes*. These are dormant genes in our bodies that absorb various external "hits" until they "switch on" and tell our cells to mutate. *Some* of us will never "turn on" our oncogenes. So the question is, are there specific genes that make us more susceptible to a carcinogen, such as tobacco or pesticides, for example?

As for specific cancer genes that are present in the sperm and eggs when we reproduce, only a small number of cancers have been shown to be inherited in this way. Most research is trying to pin down *what* switches on some oncogenes and not others.

The breast cancer gene

Several inherited abnormal genes can cause susceptibility to certain cancers, including BRCA1, BRCA2, BRCA3, hMLH1 and hMLH2. The most well known breast cancer gene that has been isolated is BRCA1, and women who have this gene are more susceptible to breast cancer than those who don't. It's possible to be screened for this gene, but doing mass screenings is not very useful because this gene accounts for only 4–5 percent of all breast cancers. It is also found in women who don't get breast cancer and who come from low-risk families. Because we don't know what finding BRCA1 in a woman without a high-risk family means, screening everyone would wind up scaring people for no good reason. In addition, there are probably many other genes—good and bad—that play a role in the development of breast cancer; we just haven't found all of them yet. Another problem with screening is that there is no way to tell a woman without the BRCA1 gene that she's *not* at risk for breast cancer because there are so many other factors involved. At this point, the reasoning is that it's better to spend this money on something that we know for a fact can save lives.

It's estimated that one in 300 women carry this gene and that it's responsible for 4 percent of all breast cancer cases. In younger women, however, the BRCA1 gene is implicated in 25 percent of cases.

What if you have the BRCA1 gene?

If you are BRCA1-positive, it's estimated, using data from high-risk families, that there is an 85-percent chance of you developing breast cancer before age 80, although about 50 percent of women who fall into this group will develop the disease before they are 50. It's also been found that women who test positive come from families in which half of all female members are affected.

The BRCA1 is a dominant gene, but in our bodies, behaves as a recessive gene. It kicks into action when its normal partner gene (which may be a tumor suppresser gene) is either lost or becomes inactive.

About genetic testing

In order to determine whether the cancer in your family is genetic, it's recommended that you and your family go for genetic counseling. This is important because predictive genetic testing is a relatively new field with few guidelines for testing, so its practitioners have little experience as a result. The counselors will document your family history to check if you say yes to any of the following statements:

1. Cancers occur in three or more family members.

2. Cancers occur before age 40.

3. A person in your family develops more than one cancer (for example, separate cancers in each breast, or ovarian and breast cancer).

4. Family members have "closely related" cancers (for example, breast, ovary, colon, endometrial, and uterus—all hormone-related). Keep in mind that with hormonal replacement therapy, where both estrogen and progestin are used after menopause, endometrial cancer can be almost completely prevented.

The implications of a positive or negative result need to be considered carefully. Again, neither result is a guarantee of cancer or no cancer in your lifetime. If necessary, a genetic counselor will recommend screening methods such as a screening mammogram or colonoscopy. Some experts recommend mammograms begin at age 25 if you're considered at high risk for breast cancer, and age 20 if your family members develop breast cancer in their 30s. Not all experts agree with these recommendations, however.

More controversy surrounds other recommendations to women with a high-risk family who also has the BRCA1 gene. Recommendations may involve a bilateral mastectomy, an oophorectomy, and taking tamoxifen as prevention therapy. The pros and cons of each of these recommendations must be thoroughly discussed with more than one cancer expert.

Mammography Guidelines at Age 50

Depending on what you read and which expert you talk to, you will probably hear two sets of mammography screening guidelines: "mammography at 50" and "mammography at age 40." The good news is that now, when you're turning age 50, the guidelines are much clearer. That's because no one disagrees with the benefits of routine breast screening at age 50.

Advocates of screening at age 50 point to the fact that breast cancer incidence (per 100,000 women) rises after age 50 (that is, after menopause), which is why screening should begin at this time. But, the truth is, *the rate of increased risk* is actually highest *until* age 50, when the rate of increase drops slightly.

Another theory is that denser breast tissue, which is *premenopausal* breast tissue (and hence, *younger* than 50), is more difficult to compress and, therefore, more difficult to read and interpret. The older the woman, the *fattier* the breast tissue is and the easier it is to read and interpret the mammogram.

Only 1/5 of all abnormalities found on mammograms turns out to be malignant. In the United States, out of the roughly 600,000 breast biopsies done per year for mammographic abnormalities, only 20–30 percent at best are actually malignant. Therefore 580,000 women will go through the emotional roller coaster associated with breast biopsies. In fact, the emotional toll of being told the mammogram is positive has actually been figured in dollars and cents and is not insignificant.

Who recommends what?

Presently, the American Cancer Society recommends that women 40 and older have annual mammograms, whereas the National Cancer Institute recommends that age group to have mammograms every one or two years. If you haven't gone yet, don't worry about it, because...

The American College of Obstetricians and Gynecologists, the American College of Radiologists, and their Canadian, British, Swedish, Dutch, and Italian counterparts recommend mammographies annually for women age 50 or older; and the American College of Physicians recommends mammograms every two years for women 50 or older. In this age group, routine mammography (every two to three years) seems to reduce annual mortality rates by 20–40 precent.

The American Medical Association, te National Cancer Institute, and The American Cancer Society *were* recommending screenings every one or two years for women 40 years and older; in light of a 1992 Canadian study (which many experts dismissed as flawed), guidelines went into flux and seem to be reverting back to screening at 50.

What should you do?

You have to make your screening decision based on your level of personal comfort. Whether you go every year, or once every two years, or not at all, it's important to check your breasts monthly for lumps. If you are "freaking out" because you think you should have been screened earlier but were not, take comfort in the fact that the science on this is inconclusive. Because your breasts radically change after menopause in terms of density, having what the American Medical Association recommends as a "baseline mammogram" sometime between ges 35 and 39 (which in theory, can be compared to future mammograms), is probably not very useful because it is only comparing melons to apples. Here are some *other* guidelines to use in sorting out what to do about mammography:

➤ Any time you find a suspicious lump, a mammography may be recommended. No matter how old you are or what your risk factors are, do so. If there's a question as to your screening center's credibility (from word of mouth, for example, or a bad experience you perceive), get a second one done at another center.

➤ If you have any family history of estrogen-dependent cancers, such as breast, ovarian, or colon cancer, earlier routine screening at 40 may be a good idea and can offer you some comfort. Many experts recommend that with this kind of history, annual screening after 40 is a good idea. If your mother, sister, or grandmother had breast cancer, you may even want to consider mammography at 35.

➤ For the rest of the population, some lifestyle and dietary adjustments discussed later are the "recipe for prevention." Then, beginning routine screening at the guideline age you're comfortable with makes the most sense.

➤ Regardless of your age, you should be doing Breast Self Examinations (BSEs) and familiarizing yourself with your breasts so you'll be equipped to notice anything unusual. (For instructions go to *www.sarahealth.com* and click on Breast Health.)You should also make sure that a manual breast exam is performed by your doctor each year with your Pap smears.

Maximizing Mammography

Outside of feeling your own breast regularly, you have to make the best of mammography, which currently carries between a 10–15 percent false negative rate and a much higher false positive rate.

Many women avoid even routine mammography beyond 50 because they fear pain, radiation, or the possibility of a positive result. But other barriers to mammography include a lack of education about when and why to have one, the lack of transportation to a screening center, language difficulties, cultural issues, and even illiteracy. Clearly, it's impossible for all of these barriers to be removed, but if you have a relative or friend, for example, who refuses to have a mammogram because of some of these barriers, you can help to educate her by translating or explaining information you, yourself, receive or by accompanying her to a physician (hers or yours) who can help explain screening to her.

How to get the most out of your mammogram:

1. Go to a reliable screening center. It should specializes in mammograms and do at least 20 to 30 mammograms per day.

2. The image of the breast on the x-ray must be of the highest quality. Good equipment used only for mammography and purchased no later than three years ago is your best bet. Cheap or older equipment used by a cut-rate center will be of no value to you. And, it could deliver false positives.

3. A dedicated, experienced technician specially trained in mammography must perform the screening. Ideally, the radiologist interpreting your mammogram should *specialize in breast radiology* (ask if he or she does). This is not as common as it is slowly *becoming.* Now, some specialists do recommend that at least two experienced *radiologists* read and interpret mammogram results. This is expensive. And if you have two radiologists who do *not* specialize in reading mammography, you're probably no farther ahead. So, ask at your mammogram facility: How many mammograms has the radiologist read? What is the facility's "call-back" record? (How many second looks does the facility do? A reasonable number is about 10 percent or less. A high call-back rate is suspicious because it suggests that the radiologist may be insecure about the readings and keeps rechecking for tiny little things. If the facility doesn't know the call-back record, go elsewhere; it's a sign that there isn't very good quality control there.)

4. For the mammogram to be as accurate as possible, there must be maximum compression on the breast, so it may hurt a little bit. Compression also reduces the amount of radiation required. Experts suggest going after your period, when your breasts are least tender. You can also take an over-the-counter painkiller an hour before the test.

5. How much time per patient is spent in that mammography room? Anything less than 20 minutes per patient is too fast!

6. A physical examination of the breasts by a trained nurse or qualified physician *must* accompany the mammogram. Before you go, however, you may want to see your doctor first, who will address any concerns he or she has on your mammogram requisition. In fact, the best places have a radiologist do the clinical exam, read the mammogram, and perform an ultrasound. That way, when it is time to interpret the mammogram, he or she has all the information components he or she needs to interpret it accurately.

7. Don't wear any talcum powder, deodorant, or lotions on your upper body the day you're scheduled. Little flecks can get on the plates and interfere with the results.

Interpreting results

Ten radiologists can have 10 different interpretations of a mammography and 10 different recommendations in terms of "what next." Variations in mammogram interpretations have to with several areas:

➢ **Visual observations.** Some radiologists can observe a lesion in a given film, whereas another may miss it altogether.

➢ **Perception.** One tumor (or "mass") may be perceived as "probably benign" by radiologist A and "probably cancerous" by radiologist B. It's the same principle as a glass half-full or half-empty. It all depends on your personality and perspective.

➢ **Concern.** Some radiologists will follow up every abnormality observed—no matter how small—with further tests; others may reserve follow-up tests for only "highly suspicious" abnormalities. Again, it depends on the personality of the radiologist looking at the film.

➢ **Variables.** These include your age, size of breasts, and medical history, and the quality of mammography equipment.

Current studies show that mammogram interpretations vary so much that many interpreters failed to identify some patients with cancer. In fact, almost 30 percent of the cancers in one study were incorrectly categorized when the films were originally interpreted. Many experts currently recommend that because radiologists differ in what they catch or miss, two observers for one mammogram may be the best route. Other experts point out that one mammographer solely specializing in breast radiology may still be better than two who do not specialize in breasts. In Sweden, where mammography interpretation and standards are considered the best in the world, two radiologists per mammogram has increased the cancer detection rate by 15 percent.

Prevention Strategies for Breast Cancer

If you're considered at "high risk" for breast cancer (and as I discussed previously, this term is meaningless, as 70 percent of women who develop breast cancer have no known risk factors), these are the prevention programs that have been "cooked up" for you. Many experts believe that making some simple lifestyle changes may be better then some of these options. And what's currently being sold to you as "prevention" may cause more health problems in the long run.

The Truth About Tamoxifen

Tamoxifen—the very same drug used to treat estrogen-receptor-positive breast cancer—was approved by the FDA in 1998 "to reduce the incidence of breast cancer in women at high risk." This is different than approving tamoxifen as a "prevention drug" for breast cancer, especially because there is no proof that tamoxifen can prevent breast cancer.

Here's how tamoxifen got approved as a prevention drug: In 1992, $68 million was allocated to the Breast Cancer Study (incorrectly referred to by the media as the "breast cancer prevention trial"). The Breast Cancer Study was conducted throughout the United States and Canada. It included 13,000 women at high risk for invasive breast cancer. Half of the women took tamoxifen (20 mg/day) and half took a placebo. The women in the study were at least 35 and had a combination of risks that made their chances of developing breast cancer relatively high. These risk factors comprised women who were over age 60, women with a family history of breast cancer, women with an early puberty, and women with a history of suspicious or benign lumps in the breast.

The women were followed for 4.2 years. In the tamoxifen group, 2.2 percent developed breast cancer, compared to 4.3 percent in the placebo group. That is why it is reported that tamoxifen can cut the risk of breast cancer "in half." What was *not* reported however, is that the numbers of deaths from breast cancer *equaled* the number of deaths from tamoxifen's side effects (endometrial cancer, blood clots, stroke, etc.). In other words, the study revealed that there was a reduction of 2.9 cases of breast cancer per 1,000 women per year (this was "the benefit"), but an increase by 2.8 cases of life-threatening side effects from tamoxifen, such as uterine cancer, blood clots, and stroke. The bottom line is that there was no difference in the overall survival rates in either group. It's important, too, to keep in mind that the benefit of tamoxifen applied only to women in this particular study, who were believed to have twice the risk of breast cancer. So women with a lower risk of breast cancer will benefit less.

We don't know if tamoxifen prevented breast cancer from occurring or if the cancers were delayed and will appear later. Because this study was too short to assess whether longer exposure to tamoxifen can cause other types of cancer to develop or to assess whether breast cancer rates might increase after women stopped taking the drug. In Europe, there are two ongoing studies with tamoxifen in women with a high risk of breast cancer. These studies have shown no difference in the number of breast cancer cases between the women who took tamoxifen and those who took a placebo.

The Breast Cancer Study also showed that the breast cancers that developed in women using tamoxifen were also the easiest ones to treat: small tumors and those that were estrogen-receptor positive. So if you're being treated with tamoxifen, it does not guarantee that it will be diagnosed at an early stage, and it docs not affect your survival. Taking tamoxifen for five years can delay the appearance of breast cancer and/or may decrease the number of tumors that will develop.

Much of the misinformation about what tamoxifen supposedly does occurs in the media. For example, *The Lehrer News Hour* presented a segment by its health reporter on Feburary 18, 1999 stating that tamoxifen prevented breast cancer. Corrections were made on air and to the PBS Website March 22 1999, after letters of complaint and protest were sent to PBS by scientists who made it clear that the results of the tamoxifen study did *not* prove, in any way, that the drug could "prevent" breast cancer.

The bottom line is that the use of tamoxifen as a prevention therapy is extremely controversial because tamoxifen is an antiestrogen drug, which means that it has side effects when given to healthy women (without any sign of breast cancer), and these side effects need to be weighed against the perceived benefits of this drug. The Breast Cancer Study revealed that life-threatening risks of tamoxifen include:

> ➢ Endometrial or uterine cancer (this occurs at a rate two to seven times greater in tamoxifen-treated women, and earlier studies show that tamoxifen-related endometrial cancer can be more severe than other forms of endometrial cancer).

> ➢ Blood clot in the lungs.

> ➢ Blood clot in the veins.

> ➢ Stroke.

> ➢ Liver cancer or liver problems.

Other side effects of tamoxifen include hot flashes, vaginal discharge or bleeding, menstrual irregularities, cataracts, color blindness, and changes in vision. Hair loss and skin rashes have also been reported, and 15 percent of women in the Breast Cancer Study stopped the drug because of the side effects.

Supporters of tamoxifen argue that although the incidence of uterine cancer doubled in the study, because uterine cancer is curable and breast cancer isn't, one is the lesser evil and worth the risk. But 1997 research presented at the World Conference on Breast Cancer and the Environment revealed that tamoxifen also increases risk of ovarian and cervical cancer and can also cause depression.

Critics of the Breast Cancer Study

Critics of this study argue that the women enrolled in it were not informed of the risks tamoxifen carried, such as menopausal symptoms and endometrial and liver cancer. The study's recruitment criteria was also criticized; 98.2 percent of all women recruited were white, coloring any meaningful data for women of other ethnic origins. In addition, the drug has not been tested in the following women:

➤ Those with less than 10 years to live.

➤ Those with a prior history of breast cancer or in whom cancer of any type was suspected.

➤ Those with existing diseases in which tamoxifen would be dangerous, such as diabetes or heart disease.

➤ Those on hormone replacement therapy (women with an intact uterus), unopposed estrogen therapy (women who have had a hysterectomy), oral contraceptives, or male hormones.

➤ Those who already took tamoxifen.

➤ Those with history of macular degeneration (eye problems).

➤ Those who refused to undergo regular sampling of their endometrial tissue.

Critics also argued that this study was rooted in profit. When tamoxifen is touted as a "prevention drug," then, in theory, one half of the female population becomes the target market. And that means someone will make plenty of money off of women's fears of breast cancer, even though there wasn't clear proof that tamoxifen can prevent breast cancer in healthy.

Research ethicists challenge the Breast Cancer Study on ethical grounds, stating that tamoxifen is not suitable as a prevention drug in presymptomatic women because:

1. It is not "relatively safe" or "free from life-threatening side effects."

2. It should be administered to women *clearly* at risk for this disease rather than to women who merely exhibit "superficial" risk *markers,* such as age or race.

3. Risk factors of the disease "should be well understood" prior to undertaking such a study.

4. The drug should be proven effective for preventing breast cancer.

Finally, critics maintain that, although tamoxifen is not many things, it is also not a *primary* prevention; it serves to further medicate healthy women instead of addressing lifestyle or behavior modifications that can reduce *exposure* to known carcinogens or mutagens. Essentially tamoxifen is seen by many as a wolf in sheep's clothing; it is aggressive treatment that is called "prevention."

Presently, Public Citizen (founded by Ralph Nader) and the National Women's Health Network issued to the FDA a Citizen's Petition to Revise the Labeling on Tamoxifen. Much of the information in this section was taken from the groups' proposed Medication Guide for patients. The Guide was proposed because both groups felt the current FDA-approved label provides inadequate information and is difficult for both patients and physicians to interpret.

Preventative Mastectomy

Doctors sometimes recommend preventative or prophylactic mastectomy. Surgeons I've interviewed tell me that when it comes to this procedure, it's the patient who wants it, rather than the doctor. Although this procedure does lower your risk, it doesn't guarantee that you'll never get breast cancer, because some breast tissue remains. These are the only scenarios where this procedure should ever be considered:

➤ Risk of bilateral, premenopausal familial breast cancer. For example, if your mother and your sister both developed bilateral invasive breast cancer at, say, age 35, you would be considered very likely to develop breast cancer around this age, too.

➤ Diagnosis of lobular carcinoma in situ (a marker for breast cancer risk) is considered a sign of higher cancer risk in either breast. Depending on your age, medical history, and family history, preventative mastectomy may be an option.

➤ Breast cancer has been diagnosed in one breast. Depending on the staging and invasiveness of the cancer, a preventative mastectomy for the other breast may be an option.

The decision to have a preventative mastectomy is highly individual. With the advent of far more sensitive mammograms (which will presumably get more sensitive as time goes on), many experts are abandoning preventative mastectomy as a strategy. If this is being recommended, you should definitely seek out a second opinion from a breast surgeon (not just a general surgeon).

A double preventive, or prophylactic, mastectomy (also called a bilateral prophylactic mastectomy) lowers your risk of breast cancer by 90 percent, but cannot 100-percent guarantee that you will never get breast cancer because some breast tissue remains.

New Advances

As of this writing, "breakthrough treatments" or possible prevention therapies for breast cancer have been exploding into medical journals and newspapers and television news reports daily. The three questions you must always ask when you read or hear about new treatments and therapies for breast cancer are:

1. **Is the treatment experimental or readily available?** Unless the treatment is "readily available" it means that many more studies, clinical trials, and experiments need to be done before the treatment is offered by a doctor near you. Also, it may mean the therapy is so expensive, no average woman with breast cancer can possibly afford it, let alone the Province, and so it will not become "standard therapy" without years of lobbying and activism.

2. **Is this new treatment of the week proven to work in human women who actually had (have) breast cancer?** Or is the hype based on animal studies or clinical trials involving a

ridiculously small sample of say, five women in a suburb? In other words, when something works in a women, there could be dozens of reasons for the drug's success that have nothing to do with the drug itself and more to do with the small sample of women (lifestyle, diet, etc.).

3. *When* **will the drug be approved or available?** How many times have you read in the newspaper or heard on the news the famous last words of a hyped report: "...but scientists say the drug is years away from approval" or "critics of the drug say many more studies are needed to prove its safety and effectiveness"? Start paying more attention to the last sentence of the article or report than the headline. Headlines that start with "Promising new therapy for breast cancer" usually end with a "But...."

What to Eat

Your greatest protection from breast cancer is modifying your diet. A heart-smart diet (see Chapter 2) combined with a colon-friendly diet (see Chapter 5) is considered "breast cancer protection" diet. By lowering the fat content in our diets, we lower the amount of fat-soluble toxins that live in our bodies. Also, the more fat we eat, the bigger our fat cells get, and the more estrogen our fat cells make—considered a risk factor for breast cancer, too. But because breast cancer is also linked to environmental chemicals, you may wish to choose organic produce.

Eating Organically

To cut down on dietary pollutants that can increase our risk of breast cancer, it's suggested that we cut down on the following:

➤ **Meat.** Most livestock is fed hormones, which we ingest. Even organically raised meat, such as free-range chicken, can still be exposed to pesticides, in the vegetation *they* ingest. These homones can wind up inside our own bodies, contributing to an estrogen overload. Meat is also, of course, higher in fat. (But because we're omnivores, our bodies are meant to eat a certain amount of meat and other animal products, good sources of iron, vitamin B12, and zinc.)

➤ **Animal products**, such as eggs.

➤ **Fish.** If you eat fish from contaminated waters, you may be ingesting mercury or PCBs, which gets stored in your fat. Otherwise, fish that is contaminant-free is quite healthy.

Before you eat:

➤ You can find out what your produce has eaten and whether it was injected with anything by calling the USDA at 202-720–2791.

➤ You can find out what waters your fish has swum in by calling the previous number.

➤ You can find "safe food" that is organically grown through a number of natural produce supermarkets.

➤ You can find out what your grown produce was sprayed with before by calling the previous number.

➤ You can find out more about your supermarket's buying habits when it comes to produce by contacting your supermarket's head office.

Plant Chemicals That Can Protect Your Breasts

➤ **Algin.** Found in brown kelp (also known as kombu or laminaria, often used as a food seasoning and wrap (for example, sushi) in soups and salads.

➤ **Bioflavonoids.** Found in fresh fruits, vegetables, and other greens, especially deeply colored produce (for example, orange squash, and blueberries).

- **Carotenoids.** Found in apricots (including dried), carrots, collard greens, kale, spinach, sweet potatoes, tomatoes, pumpkin, and watermelon.

- **Fiber.** Found in all organic whole grains, fruits, and vegetables.

- **Flavonoids.** Found in deeply colored fruits, especially blueberries, huckleberries, oranges, lemons, strawberries, green and red peppers, and broccoli.

- **Indole 3-carbinol.** Found in cruciferous vegetables (broccoli, cabbage, cauliflower).

- **Phytoestrogens.** Found in soy products.

- **Selenium.** Found in brewer's yeast, garlic, organic whole grains, safe seafood (tuna, shellfish); supplements combining selenium with garlic work synergistically.

- **Sulfur-rich amino acids.** Found in garlic.

- **Sulforaphane.** Found in bok choy, broccoli, and cauliflower.

- **Vitamin C.** Found in broccoli, cauliflower, citrus fruits, and peppers.

- **Tocopherols.** Found in vegetable oils, almonds, soybeans, sunflower seeds, wheat germ, and wheat germ oil.

Immune Boosters

Today, many substances, such as echinacea and zinc, are as popular as vitamin C. Here's an overview of some of the well-known immune boosters, which means they stimulate your immune system or strengthen it to help fight diseases such as cancer:

- **Echinacea.** This is a flower that belongs to the sunflower family. It's believed that echinacea increases the number of cells in your immune system to fight off disease.

- **Essiac.** This is a mixture of four herbs comprising Indian rhubarb, sheepshead sorrel, slippery elm, and burdock root.

Essiac is believed to strengthen the immune system, improve appetite, supply essential nutrients to the body, possibly relieve pain, and, ultimately, prolong life.

➤ **Ginseng.** This is a root used in Chinese medicine, but it's believed to enhance your immune system and boost the activity of white blood cells.

➤ **Green Tea.** This is a popular Asian tea made from a plant called *Camellia sinensis.* The active chemical in green tea is epigallocatechin gallate (EGCG). It is believed that green tea neutralizes free radicals, which are carcinogenic. It is considered to be an anticancer tea—particularly for stomach, lung, and skin cancers.

➤ **Iscador** (a.k.a. mistletoe). Iscador is made through a fermentation process, using different kinds of mistletoe, a plant known for its white berries. More popular as an anti-tumor treatment in Europe, it's believed that Iscador works by enhancing your immune system and inhibiting tumor growth.

➤ **Paul d'Arco** (a.k.a. Taheebo). This usually comes in the form of a tea made from the inner bark of a tree called Tabebuia. It's believed to a cleansing agent and can be used as an antimicrobial agent and is said to stop tumor growth.

➤ **Wheatgrass.** This is grass grown from wheatberry seeds, which are rich in chlorophyll. Its juice contains more than 100 vitamins, minerals, and nutrients, and is believed to contain a number of cancer-fighting agents and immune-boosting properties.

The following spices are said to be anti-cancer agents. Use some of the spices on this list in your next meal:

Neem flowers.	Tumeric.	Onions.
Parsley.	Black pepper.	Asfetida.
Pippali.	Garlic.	Kandathiipile.
Ponnakanni.	Cumin and poppy seeds.	

Mananthakkali, drumstick, and basil leaves.

How to Move

By following the guidelines under "How To Move" in Chapters 2 and 3, you can help lower your risk of breast cancer. In addition, deep-breathing exercises can help to stimulate oxygen flow and your immune system. But the best movements of all when it comes to breast health is to feel your breasts for changes or lumps, outlined under Breast Self Exam (BSE).

BSE: Breast Self-Examination

This method should be called "get to know your breasts." It involves specific steps of feeling your breast at the same time each month and distinguishing suspicious lumps from normal lumpy/bumpy breasts. In addition, you can't know if a lump has remained "unchanged" unless you've been checking your breasts monthly.

While you're still menstruating, you'll need to do a BSE after your period ends when your breasts are least tender and lumpy. When you're pregnant, BSEs should be done monthly throughout all stages of your pregnancy. When you're breastfeeding, perform BSEs on a monthly basis after a feeding, when your breasts aren't filled with milk. (And then, after your periods return, perform BSEs after a feeding, *after* your period!) If you're past menopause, just pick the same time each month, such as the first or 15th of the month to do it.

Although the steps of a BSE follow, make sure your doctor actually *shows* you how to do it as well. In addition, there is a kit available through the National Cancer Institute called the *Mammacare Learning System*, which consists of a 45-minute video and a 30-page instructional manual. This kit was designed to teach you how to do a breast self-exam using what is known as a "vertical grid pattern," currently the most effective pattern. The kit was developed at the University of Florida and was partially funded by the National Cancer Institute.

At any rate, here are the steps to BSE:

1. Visually inspect your breasts. Stand in front of the mirror and look closely at your breasts. You're looking for dimpling, puckering (like an orange peel in appearance), or noticeable lumps. Do you see any discharge that dribbles out on its own or bleeding from the nipple? Any funny dry patches on the nipple (which may be Paget's disease)?

2. Visually inspect your breasts with your arms raised. Now, raise your arms over your head and in front of the mirror, and look for the same things. Raising your arms smoothes out the breast a little more so these changes are more obvious.

3. Palpation (feeling your breast). Lie down on your bed with a pillow under your left shoulder and place your left hand under your head. With the flat part of the fingertips of your right hand, examine your left breast for a lump, using a gentle circular motion. Imagine that the breast is a clock, and make sure you feel each "hour," as well as the nipple area and armpit area.

4. *Repeat step 3, but reverse sides, examining your right breast with your left hand.*

5. *If you find a lump:* Note the size, the shape, and how painful it is. A suspicious lump is usually painless and about 1/4–1/2 inch in size and remains unchanged from month to month. Get your lump looked at as soon as you can, or if you're comfortable doing so, wait for the next cycle/month. If the lump changes in the next cycle by shrinking or *becoming* painful, it's not cancerous, but should be looked at anyway. If the suspicious lump stays the same, definitely get it looked at as soon as possible. Keep in mind that breast cysts are common, vary in size, and are occasionally tender.

6. *If discharge oozes out of your nipple on its own, or if blood comes out,* see your doctor immediately. Don't wait.

7. *If your nipple is dry and patchy,* see your doctor immediately. Don't wait.

Stretches Good for Your Breasts

➤ Chest Expander: Stand with feet hip width apart, arms resting comfortably at your side. Gently allow your arms to drift backwards, until you can claps your hands behind you. Exhale, keeping your body aligned while you stretch your arms behind you. Breathe deeply and hold.

➤ Cobra (Upward Facing Dog): Lie on your belly with your palms down and adjacent to your shoulders. Slowly raise your upper body, lifting all but the lower abdomen toward the ceiling. Breathe deeply. Release.

➤ Child's Pose: Sit on your heels. Bring your forehead to the floor in front of you. Breathe into the back of the ribcage, feeling the stretch in your spine. Hold as long as it's comfortable.

➤ Surrender Squeeze: Clasp your hands in front of you as if in prayer. Slowly move your hands backward to squeeze your shoulder blades together. Hold for 10 seconds, breathing deeply.

➤ Neurolymphatic points for Breast Pain and Chest Soreness: The lymphatics are tiny vessels that carry waste products from the body's peripherals to the neck area, where they empty into the veins leading to the heart.

Colon Health

Keeping your colon healthy is the key to avoiding a number of health problems from head to toe, including obesity, heart disease, and a variety of cancers, including, of course colon and rectal cancer. Many women don't realize that colon cancer strikes slightly more women than men, especially beyond the age of 45. And many women don't realize that colon cancer is almost 90 percent preventable through diet, exercise, and regular screenings.

Staying Regular

The colon essentially acts as a solid waste container, drying out the waste that doesn't get absorbed further up. Our nervous system controls the muscular contractions of your colon, which slowly moves your waste downward, toward your rectum. We experience these stronger muscular contractions as "the urge." And once we feel the urge, we sit down, relax, and allow the gentle contractions to overtake us. All we have to do is relax and the anal sphincter will open to allow the passage of stool.

The frequency of bowel movements varies from person to person. Although many North American sources say it's "normal" to move your bowels anywhere from a few times per day to a few times per week, if you're not having one to three large, bulky, soft but firm bowel movements per day, you probably have a tendency to be constipated. A normal stool is solid or "formed" but not hard, and certainly should not contain mucus or blood. The stools should pass without cramps, pain, or strain. However, normal stools can pass noisily, because natural gas (called flatus)—swallowed air (nitrogen) that gets trapped in the lower intestine—often comes out with the stool or independently.

Constipation

Constipation means that you are not experiencing an urge to move your bowels, and when you do the stools are hard and difficult to pass. Generally, if more than three days have passed since your last bowel movement, the stools will harden. The colon will continue to dry out the stools because that's what colons do.

Most constipation is "functional" in that there is no disease or organic problem at work; it's a lifestyle problem, having to do with ignoring the urge to go (if you're surrounded by public toilets, for example) or not allowing enough time in the morning to *create* the urge to go by drinking or eating something. If you ignore the urge too often, you may stop feeling an urge altogether. Studies comparing bowel habits of North Americans to Africans show that the incidence of colon cancer is higher in North Americans, who have less frequent bowel movements than Africans. We can learn from these studies and modify our lifestyles accordingly. The idea is to find a happy medium, because chronic diarrhea is also dangerous to your health. In fact, it's far more troublesome than chronic constipation.

By simply obeying your urges, you can avoid constipation. Learning to suppress the urge to defecate can create what is called a "lazy bowel." When you feel the urge to defecate, drop what you're doing and get to the toilet. We all know ways of excusing ourselves to make or take "important calls." Why not make your nature call the most important call of your day?

Another way to obey the nature call is to give yourself enough time to receive the call in the first place. If you get out of bed and rush out the door immediately, you may be one of millions who suffer from "commuter constipation."

If your constipation is a more sudden or recent occurrence in your life, then there could be other causes, such as:

➤ **Hypothyroidism** (low-functioning thyroid). Request a thyroid stimulating hormone test (TSH) to check for thyroid function, if you suspect this.

➤ **Pregnancy or changes in the menstrual cycle.** It's not unusual for women to experience constipation at these times.

➤ **Hot weather.** When you're perspiring and losing body fluid, you could become constipated.

➤ **Stress.** This is often the cause (see "Commuter Constipation").

➤ **Travel.** (Changes in schedule, diet, and time zones can interfere with regularity.)

➤ **Anal sores** (including fissures, hemorrhoids, or herpes).

➤ **Medications** (particularly pain control medications in chronic illness).

➤ **Periods of vomiting and diarrhea.**

Chronic constipation

Chronic constipation can be caused by a variety of things, including laxative abuse, diseases affecting body tissues, nerve or muscle control, inflammation, scarring or blockage in the lower intestine, spinal injuries, prolonged bedrest, or being bedridden (especially seniors). But again, lack of exercise and poor diet are the most common causes of chronic constipation.

Hemorrhoids

The straining caused by chronic constipation can lead to hemorrhoids. These are swollen blood vessels or veins around the anus inside (internal) covered by the inner lining. A classic symptom of internal hemorrhoids is finding bright red blood squirting into the toilet water, covering your stool, on toilet paper, or in the toilet bowl. Sometimes an internal hemorrhoid is large enough that it protrudes through your rectum and hangs outside the body, known as a *protruding hemorrhoid*. Because bleeding is a problem with internal hemorrhoids, you can become anemic.

To find some relief, try warm tub or sitz baths (the water should just cover your rear end) several times a day. Don't use anything in the water except a little baking soda (optional), and don't stay in longer than about 10 minutes. Stool softeners may help you pass stool more comfortably, and ice packs will help reduce swelling (10 minutes on/10 minutes off). Frequently shifting your positions while standing or sitting is helpful. Over-the-counter medication, such as Preparation H, can also give you relief but won't shrink the hemorrhoid. If the problem is not resolving itself, the hemorrhoid can be removed in your doctor's office.

The Trouble With Laxatives

The best way to know the "right" laxatives is to know the *wrong* ones. What you want to avoid is anything that is a *stimulant laxative*, which can include "herbal" laxatives, such as senna and cascara sagrada. There is some contradictory information regarding cascara sagrada, however. Many herbalists maintain that cascara sagrada, unlike senna, is considered more of a "tonic" than a laxative, is said not to create a dependency, and, in fact, may be helpful for your colon. However, like other stimulant laxatives, it works by stimulating the colon to contract, creating a bowel movement and, with too much use, a dependency. The medical advisor for this book *strongly advises against* cascara sagrada. A dependency on laxatives means that you will not be able to move your bowels without the laxative because your colon becomes "used" to it.

There are several herbal teas and herbal concoctions that promote digestion and regularity through harmless spices or ingredients.

If you must have an occasional laxative, the best kind are bulking agents, which are sold as laxatives but are actually not a laxative per se. Metamucil is an example of a bulking agent. Adopting a "water with fiber routine" (see page 146) will probably cure you of constipation. Try that first before you try a laxative. If nothing is working, and you haven't moved your bowels in five to six days, insert a glycerin suppository overnight and in the morning, to get things moving. If there's still no action, the next step is to try an enema and, after that, a mild laxative, such as milk of magnesia. Finally, you may have a bowel obstruction of some sort, which a good gastroenterologist can uncover.

Retraining Your Bowels

For many, years of ignoring our urges and laxative dependency have made it impossible to "go it alone." Take heart: You can retrain your bowel and recapture its youth. Here's the recipe:

> ➤ Drink a glass of warm water in the morning as soon as you get up, and insert a glycerin suppository into your rectum.

> ➤ Move around a bit (make your bed, do some stretches, etc.) for about 3 or 4 minutes.

> ➤ Sit on the toilet and gently push for about two minutes. If nothing happens, get up.

If you practice this routine every day for three to six months, then you should be able to train your colon to have a bowel movement when you drink warm water in the morning.

In other words, the warm water will stimulate your colon. Missing even a day of this routine could set you back weeks, though!

Bowel Diseases

Bowel diseases can plague women of all ages, but they can become aggravated as we age. This section addresses two common bowel conditions that affect women: irritable bowel syndrome and inflammatory bowel disease.

Irritable Bowels?

A most confusing label is in vogue, which defines the bowel habits of between 25 and 55 million North Americans, two-thirds of which are women. The label is *irritable bowel syndrome* (IBS), which refers to unusual bowel "patterns" that alternate between diarrhea and constipation, and everything in between. IBS is also referred to as: irritable or spastic colon; spastic, mucus, nervous, laxative, cathartic, or functional colitis; spastic bowel; nervous indigestion; functional dyspepsia; pylorospasm; and functional bowel disease. The problem with using the term *irritable* is that irritation is *not* what's occuring. It also sounds too much like *inflammatory*, which is not what's going on, either. Worse, many family doctors will say "IBS" instead of "I don't know what's going on—but have you tried fiber?"

The term *irritable* bowel syndrome came into use to describe a bowel that is overly sensitive to normal activity. In other words, when the nerve endings that line the bowel are too sensitive the nerves controlling the gastrointestinal tract can become overactive, making the bowel overly responsive or "irritable" to normal things, such as passing gas or fluid. The bowel may want to pass a stool before it is time to. However, because we tend to think of irritable, when used clinically, as something that is red, irritated, or inflamed, this label is more confusing than defining. IBS has nothing to do with irritation, inflammation, or any organic disease process. It has to do with *nerves.*

The term IBS also implies that a diagnosis of your symptoms has been made and there is a definite cause—and cure—for your condition. This is not the case. IBS is a diagnosis made in the absence of any other diagnosis. There are no tests to confirm IBS, only tests to rule out other causes for your symptoms. The term *functional bowel disorder* is beginning to catch on instead of IBS because functional means that there is no disease. Yet, no matter what you call it, roughly half of all digestive disorders are attributed to IBS. After the common cold, IBS is the chief cause of absenteeism. Many doctors compare IBS to "asthma" in that there are number of causes with the same outcome. For example, asthma may be related to allergies or a hundred other things. Similarly, IBS has many different causes that are difficult to pin down. However, stress and dietary factors are the chief causes.

IBS Symptoms

IBS symptoms are characterized by frequent, violent episodes of diarrhea that will almost always strike around a stressful situation. More than 60 percent of IBS sufferers report that their symptoms first coincided with stressful life events, and 40–60 percent of people with IBS also suffer from anxiety disorders or depression, compared to 20 percent of people with other gastrointestinal disorders. Stressful life events that can bring on IBS include the death of a loved one, separation/ divorce, unresolved conflict or grief, and moving to a new city or job, as well as having a history of childhood physical or sexual abuse.

Many people will find that their symptoms will persist well beyond the stressful life event, and the episodes will invade their normal routine. There need not be one, single stressful event that precipitates IBS; it could first present itself after you've been in a stressful job for long period of time or subjected to the normal stresses of "life in North America." The episodes of diarrhea are often accompanied by crampy, abdominal pains or gas, which are relieved by a bowel movement. The pain may shift around in the abdomen as well. After the diarrhea episodes, you may then be plagued by long bouts of constipation, or the feeling that you're not emptying your bowels completely when you do go. Again, IBS refers to an irregular bowel *pattern* rather than one particular episode. The pattern is that there is no *normal* pattern of bowel movements; it is often one extreme or the other.

Your stool may also contain mucus, which can make the stool long and rope-like or worm-like. The mucus is normally secreted by the colon to help the stool along in a normal movement. With IBS, your colon secretes too much mucus.

Blood mixed with your stool means this is *not IBS*, but something else. Some people can also suffer from solely diarrhea, or solely gas and constipation. Other symptoms include bloating, nausea, and loss of appetite. Fever, weight loss, or severe pain is NOT a sign of IBS but of something else.

Many people find it confusing that IBS can cause both constipation and diarrhea, which seem to be opposite ends of the spectrum. Instead of the slow muscular contractions that normally move the bowels, spasms occur, which can either result in an "explosion" or a "blockage." It's akin to a sudden gust of wind: it can blow the door wide open (diarrhea) or blow it shut (constipation). It all depends on the wind.

It's important to note the timing of your diarrhea; with IBS, your sleep should not be disturbed by it. The episodes will always occur either after a meal or in the early evening.

Factors that distinguish IBS from infectious diarrhea or inflammatory bowel diseases are:

> Finding relief through defecation.

> Noticing looser stools when the bowel movement is precipitated by pain.

> Noticing more frequent bowel movements when you experience pain.

> Noticing abdominal bloating or distention.

> Noticing mucus in the stools.

> Feeling that you have not completely emptied your bowels.

What to rule out

The symptoms of IBS are a little vague because they can be signs of many other problems. Therefore, before you accept a diagnosis of IBS, make sure your doctor has taken a careful history to investigate:

> Dietary culprits, food allergies, lactose intolerance, or just plain "poor diet" (high fats/starch; low fiber).

> Intestinal bacterial, viral, or parasitic infections. (Where have you been traveling? What are your sexual habits?)

> Overgrowth of *C. difficile*, a common cause of infectious diarrhea.

> Yeast in the gastrointestinal tract (called candidiasis), which is notorious for causing IBS symptoms. (Eating yogurt every day should clear this up.)

> Medications.

> Gastrointestinal disorders such as dysmotility (where the stomach muscles are not moving properly, causing bloating, nausea, and other problems).

➤ Enzyme deficiencies (the pancreas may not be secreting enough enzymes to break down your food).

➤ Serious disease such as Inflammatory Bowel Disease or signs of cancer.

Stress and IBS

It's possible to have a pristine diet and rule out all forms of organic disease, yet still suffer from IBS while under stress. In the same way that you can sweat, blush, or cry under emotional stress, your gastrointestinal tract may also react to stress by "weeping"—producing excessive water and mucus, overreacting to normal stimuli such as eating. What often happens, however, is that there is a delayed "gut reaction" to stress, and you may not experience your IBS symptoms until your stress has passed. Apparently, under stress your brain becomes more active as a "defense." (For example, when we're running away from a predator, we have to think quickly and act quickly, so our heart rates increase, we sweat more, and so on). During this "defensive mode" the entire nervous system can become exaggerated (that's what causes "butterflies in the stomach"). The nerves controlling the gastrointestinal tract therefore become highly sensitive, which can cause IBS symptoms. Studies show, for example, that IBS symptoms are more common on weekday mornings than afternoons or weekends, and IBS symptoms do not appear at night while sleeping.

Women and IBS

Why is IBS more common in women? First, women menstruate and experience normal mood fluctuations related to their natural menstrual cycles. As women reach menopause and the cycle becomes more erratic, so too can the bowel, as it can be stimulated by uterine contractions. The first day of a woman's period is often a day where she has several loose bowel movements. (If you recall, common symptoms of labor is diarrhea and vomiting. This occurs because of the intensity of the uterine contractions, which create "ripples" throughout the gastrointestinal tract.)

Finally, women are much more prone to eating disorders and laxative abuse, as well as domestic abuse (resulting in continuous emotional upset and stress), all of which wreak havoc on the gastrointestinal tract.

Inflammatory Bowel Disease

This is a serious, chronic condition that can be life-threatening in extreme cases. IBD is when parts (one or more) of your small or large intestine are inflamed, causing symptoms that range from unpleasant but manageable to severe and debilitating.

When inflammation and/or ulceration is confined to the inner lining of the colon (colitis) and rectum (proctitis) you have what's known as *ulcerative colitis,* which is confined to the colon and not small bowel. The inflammation will usually start in the rectum and may spread throughout the colon. Because it's inflamed, the colon will not be able to do what it was designed to do: hold your solid waste. As a result, it will need to empty waste as soon as it receives it; you'll experience this as diarrhea. The inflammation will cause the cells that line the colon to slough off or die, which may cause open sores on the lining (ulcers), which could then form pus or mucus. So the diarrhea is often tinged with blood, pus, or mucus.

When the inflammation goes beyond the lining into the actual walls of the intestine, you have what's known as *Crohn's disease,* which usually attacks a part of the gastrointestinal (GI) tract above the colon, in the ileum. For this reason, Crohn's disease is also known as ileitis or regional enteritis. But Crohn's disease can also attack the colon and/or other parts of the gastrointestinal tract.

If your intestines were a trench coat, ulcerative colitis would be confined to the lining of the coat below the belt, or *ileum*; that is, the lining of the colon and rectum. Crohn's disease would affect the *entire coat* starting at the belt, and possibly all the way up to the collar (the upper GI tract). Or it could start at the belt and affect everything below it (the lower GI tract). Think of the belt as the official separation between the upper and lower GI tract.

The risk of colon cancer is about 32 times higher if you have ulcerative colitis. That's because ulcerative colitis can cause the cells that line the colon to become precancerous (known as *dysplasia*). If only your rectum or lower part of the colon is involved, then your risk is not any higher than in the general population. Nevertheless, if you've had ulcerative colitis for more than eight years, you should be screened *annually* for evidence of dysplasia through sigmoidoscopy or colonoscopy. Tissue biopsies can be obtained through colonoscopy. If dysplasia is found, you may be offered the option of a colectomy (surgical removal of the colon) to prevent the spread of precancerous cells and the development of full-blown colon cancer.

Ulcerative Colitis

Indeed, you may have ulcerative colitis and are at an increased risk of colon cancer, but never have been officially diagnosed with this condition. So here are the symptoms that may indicate ulcerative colitis:

Abdominal cramps combined with bloody diarrhea (which could contain mucus and/or pus) and frequent, *urgent* bowel movements are the most common signs of ulcerative colitis. The diarrhea usually strikes immediately after meals or at night. Some people may also lose control of their bowel movements (called fecal incontinence) or pass stool in the belief that it is just gas. Obviously, these symptoms can interfere with many of your daily activities, including sleeping. Not all people will suffer from severe symptoms. It really depends on where the inflammation is. Sometimes it's confined to the rectum, or one side of the colon vs. the entire colon.

Yet when symptoms *are* severe, you can suffer from all of the following:

> ➤ Fatigue.

> ➤ Weight loss.

> ➤ Loss of appetite and/or nausea.

> ➤ Rectal bleeding.

> ➤ Malnutrition (mainly due to the loss of fluids and nutrients).

> ➤ Anemia (from bleeding).

The same causes that trigger your immune system to attack your bowel tissue can also cause it to attack other body tissues, causing what's known as "complications" such as skin lesions, arthritis, inflammation of the eyes, or liver disorders (including jaundice and cirrhosis), which could necessitate a liver transplant.

In severe but rare cases, the colon enlarges and distends, known as *toxic megacolon*. This will cause fever, abdominal pain, dehydration, and malnutrition. In this case, surgery is necessary to prevent the colon from rupturing.

Crohn's Disease

The symptoms of Crohn's disease are similar to ulcerative colitis: abdominal cramps and diarrhea, resulting in rectal bleeding, anemia, weight loss, and fever (fever is not usually a symptom in ulcerative colitis unless the colon enlarges). The fever may make it easy for Crohn's disease to be confused with infectious diarrhea. The location of the abdominal cramping in Crohn's disease is usually in your lower right side. Because

Crohn's disease attacks the intestinal walls and can occur higher up the gastrointestinal tract, obstruction can take place due to narrowing of passageways (they swell and develop scar tissue). Fistulas ("ulcer tunnels" between tissues) can develop around the bladder, rectum, anus, or vagina. These tunnels can become infected and filled with pus. They are a common complication and often are associated with pockets of infection or abscesses (infected areas of pus).

And, as with ulcerative colitis, the autoimmune nature of Crohn's disease can also cause other body parts to inflame, including joints, skin, eyes, and mouth. Kidney stones and gallstones are also a complication related to Crohn's.

Getting an accurate diagnosis

Because the symptoms of both ulcerative colitis and Crohn's are virtually indistinguishable, the only way to tell which disease you have is to examine your bowel tissue under a microscope. This is done by a pathologist (a doctor who specializes in analyzing tissue specimens under a microscope). There are even pathologists who subspecialize in gastroenterology. A G.I. specialist can get a tissue sample through a procedure known as sigmoidoscopy or a colonoscopy.

Your doctor will also want to collect a stool sample to rule out infections or parasites, which can also cause mucus- or pus-tinged diarrhea. And finally, blood tests will confirm whether you're anemic or have a high white blood cell count (a sign of inflammation).

Screening for Colon Cancer

Colorectal cancer (cancer in the colon and/or rectum) accounts for roughly 13 percent of all cancers and is considered the second leading cause of cancer deaths, next to lung cancer. Colorectal cancer develops from an earlier, benign growth, known as a polyp. *All colon cancer comes from polyps, but not all polyps become colon cancer.* What this means is that by screening for polyps on a regular basis, you can "catch" colon cancer before it ever develops. Think of polyps screening—or polyps hunting, as I call it—as the "Pap test" for colon cancer. In the same way that most women will be spared a diagnosis of cervical cancer, thanks to the Pap test, most people who go for regular polyp screening should be spared a diagnosis of colon cancer. Even if you are diagnosed with colorectal cancer, it's important to keep in mind that colorectal cancers develop in glandular tissue, but are considered very treatable when caught in an early stage.

Colon cancer can also be preventable through diet. Of all the studies done on cancer and dietary fat, the strongest connections can be made between high-fat diets and colon cancer. In other words, people who consume high quantities of fat have higher rates of colon cancer. People who consume low quantities of fat have lower rates of colon cancer.

As for fiber, studies show that people who consume high quantities of fiber have lower rates of colon cancer, wheras people who consume low quantities of fiber have higher rates of colon cancer. In addition, people who are regular have lower incidences of colon cancer than people who are chronically constipated. (See "What to Eat," page 142.)

The purpose of screening for colon cancer is to hunt down colon cancer "seedlings" known as polyps. Polyps are benign growths, which can develop into colon cancer. The relationship between colon cancer and polyps is similar to the relationship between a caterpillar and a butterfly. We know that all butterflies come from caterpillars, but not all caterpillars turn into butterflies; a lot of them become moths! If we wanted to eliminate all the butterflies from this planet, the best plan would be to hunt down caterpillars. Well, same thing here. The purpose of screening is to go "polyp hunting." Along the way, other diseases of the lower intestine may be detected as well, such as ulcerative colitis (see further on).

Screening Guidelines

Anyone age 45 or older is at an increased risk for colorectal cancer (colon and/or rectal) cancer, although it occurs in people who are 30-something, occasionally. In the general population, one in 20 people without any known risk factors for colorectal cancer will develop it. Known risk factors for colorectal cancer include a history of ulcerative colitis, a family history of colorectal cancer, a history of benign tumors in the colon or rectum (called polyps), a diet high in fat and low in fiber, and possibly a family history of breast or ovarian cancers (but this is hotly debated). Annual screening is recommended by age 45, or even younger.

No matter how old you are or how recently you've been screened for evidence of colon cancer, there are certain "red flag" symptoms that warrant an immediate investigation by a specialist, called either a colorectal surgeon or a gastroenterologist. The word that characterizes alarming symptoms from chronic symptoms is *sudden*. If you're between the ages of 45 and 55 and you suddenly notice the onset of any of the following symptoms, don't wait and see what happens. Get yourself to a doctor's office as soon as possible, where you can be referred for testing or to a specialist.

Symptoms that indicate a more serious illness, such as cancer, include:

➤ Changes in bowel habits.

➤ Changes in stool consistency.

➤ Black stool or dark red blood in the stool (black stools indicate bleeding from the stomach; dark red blood in the stool means the bleeding is from the lower intestine).

➤ Anemia (could mean that you're bleeding from your gastrointestinal tract).

➤ Persistent abdominal pain (that is, nothing makes it go away).

➤ New and unusual symptoms (particularly if you're between 45 and 50 or over 65).

➤ Weight loss (you've lost at least five to10 lbs. in the last month without trying).

The Appropriate Tests

You should request the following exams as part of your annual physical:

➤ **Visual examination of your rectal area.** Here, your doctor looks for visible signs of irritation or inflammation in that area.

➤ **Digital rectal exam.** This is the one where a doctor puts on the ol' rubber gloves, lubricates the fingers, and sticks his/her finger right up there to feel for unusual things: swelling, the state of your "sphincter muscles," and tenderness, which could be a sign of anal fissures, or inflammation. In women, the cervix, a bit of the uterus, and a condition known as rectocele (where the rectum bulges slightly into the vagina) can be checked. Anyone engaging in regular anal sex should have this exam annually, too.

➤ **Anoscope exam.** Here, a short lighted tube similar to, but much shorter than, a sigmoidoscope, is inserted to look for signs of inflammation or polyps growth. That said, because a sigmoidoscopy is much more accurate, many specialists recommend you skip this and go directly to sigmoidoscopy.

➤ **Occult blood test.** Also known as Fecal Occult Blood Test (FOBT), this is a test that checks for "hidden" blood in the stools (occult means "hidden"). You collect your own stool samples from three bowel movements in a row. If blood is found in the stool samples, you'll be referred for a colon-oscopy. Certain things in your diet, certain medications, or the presence of hemorrhoids could give you false positive results. This test detects less than 10 percent of small polyps, 30–50 percent of large polyps, and 40–50 percent of early-stage colorectal cancers. In other words, it may not detect the presence of polyps or cancer.

➤ **Sigmoidoscopy.** Here, a short tube with a lighted microscope on the end is inserted about 6 inches into your rectum. The lining of your colon can be examined this way, and any inflammation and polyps (a growth which can be benign or malignant) can be seen. Some doctors use a flexible sigmoidscope, which is longer (about 2 feet), but because a colonoscope reveals more, there's not much point. This test detects 30–45 percent of small polyps and 35–50 percent of large polyps or early-stage cancers.

➤ **Colonoscopy.** (Alternate every year between this and the sigmoidoscopy.) Prior to this test, you'll need to be "cleaned out" with laxatives and a liquid diet so the field of vision is clear. Done under sedation, here, a long fiber-optic, lighted tube is inserted into the colon. The tube is about 165 cm long. This enables the doctor to view all sides of the colon, looking for polyps, inflammation, and so on, and allows growths to be removed during the procedure—a particular bonus. A more effective and newer colonoscope is a video colonoscope with allows a clearer view (in color) on video. More polyps are found this way than with a fiber-optic colonoscope. This detects a whopping 85 percent of small polyps and about 97 percent of large polyps and early stage cancers.

A word about barium enemas

In light of far more accurate screening tools, such as sigmoidoscopy and colonoscopy, barium enemas are fast becoming the dinosaurs in colon cancer screening. You still need to be "cleaned out" via laxatives and a liquid diet the night before, but it may be harder to get your bowel movements back to normal after the test because the barium can dry out in the colon and become as hard as concrete. All in all, the black-and-white, two-dimensional images produced by barium X-ray are simply not as accurate as those seen in 3-D color via colonoscopy or sigmoidoscopy. And you are exposed to a small amount of radiation to boot. Because the test is expensive and the results of this test may be inconclusive, if not inaccurate—which would warrant colonoscopy anyway—most experts today say skip the barium X-ray and go directly to colonoscopy.

Genetic Testing for Colon Cancer

Yes, you can be tested for a "colon cancer gene" but the presence of a genetic mutation for colon cancer does not mean you will get colon cancer, nor does the *absence* of a genetic mutation mean that you will *not* get colon cancer. Therefore, genetic screening for colon cancer is not meaningful information for most people. And the stress a positive test can generate may cause more harm than good! If you do test positive for one of the types of colon cancer genes (or, more accurately, genetic mutations), you are encouraged to screen more frequently than people who do not have a genetic mutation for colon cancer.

Colon Cancer Genes

There is one type of colon cancer that does not originate from polyps, known as Hereditary Non-Polyposis Colorectal Cancer (HNPCC). This is a hereditary colorectal cancer that strikes at about age 45. People with this gene may also be more at risk for cancer of the uterus, bladder or ureter (the orifice out of which we urinate), pancreas, and stomach. Roughly 5 percent of colorectal cancer is due to an HNPCC gene mutation.

A second gene mutation has been discovered in roughly 6 percent of the Ashkenazi Jewish population (Jews of Eastern European descent). If you are not Jewish, it is exceedingly rare to test positive for this second kind of mutation.

Finally, less than 1 percent of colon cancer, known as Familial Adenomatous Polyposis (FAP), which is characterized by hundreds of polyps, is linked to a rare genetic mutation.

The same ethical dilemmas over genetic testing for breast cancer present themselves when looking at genetic testing for colon cancer. Review Chapter 3, page 101 for this discussion.

What to Eat

By lowering fat and increasing fiber, you'll greatly reduce your risk of colon cancer, while maintaining good colon health. In fact, experts muse that by simply following the low-fat/high-fiber diet, you may be able to avoid 90 percent of all stomach and colon cancers and 20 percent of gallbladder, pancreas, mouth, pharynx, and esophageal cancers. Diet may even play a role in preventing lung cancer; recent studies show that people with low intakes of carotene (orange, red, and purple plant foods) have higher rates of lung cancer.

Insoluble Fiber

Fiber is the part of a plant your body can't digest, which comes in the form of both water-soluble fiber (which dissolves in water) and water-insoluble fiber (which does not dissolve in water but instead, absorbs water). This is what's meant by "soluble" and "insoluble" fiber. Soluble and insoluble fiber do differ, but they are equally beneficial.

Soluble fiber, discussed in Chapter 2, somehow lowers the "bad" cholesterol (LDL) in your body. Insoluble fiber doesn't affect your cholesterol levels at all, but it regulates your bowel movements. How does it do this? As the insoluble fiber moves through your digestive tract, it absorbs water thw way a sponge does and helps to form your waste into a solid form faster, making the stools larger, softer, and easier to pass. Without insoluble fiber, your solid waste just gets pushed down to the colon or lower intestine as always, where it is stored and dried out until you're ready to have a bowel movement. High-starch foods are associated with drier stools. This is exacerbated when you "ignore the urge," as the colon will dehydrate the waste even more until it becomes harder and difficult to pass, known as constipation. Insoluble fiber will help to regulate your bowel movements by speeding things along. Insoluble fiber increases the "transit time" by increasing colon motility and limiting the time dietary toxins "hang around" the intestinal wall. This is why it can dramatically decrease your risk of colon cancer. As insoluble fiber moves through your digestive tract, it absorbs water the way a sponge and helps your stools form faster, which makes them softer, and easier to pass.

Good sources of insoluble fiber are wheat bran and whole grains, skins from various fruits and vegetables, seeds, leafy greens, and cruciferous vegetables (cauliflower, broccoli, or brussels sprouts).

What's in a grain?

Most of us will turn to grains and cereals to boost our fiber intake, which experts recommend should be at about 25–35 grams per day. Use this chart to help gauge whether you're getting enough. The following list measures the amount of insoluble fiber. If you're a little under "par," an easy way to boost your fiber intake is to simply add pure wheat bran to your foods, which is available in health food stores or supermarkets in a sort of "saw dust" format. Three tablespoons of wheat bran is equal to 4.4 grams of fiber. Sprinkle one or two tablespoons onto cereals, rice, pasta, or meat dishes. You can also sprinkle it into orange juice or low-fat yogurt. It has virtually no calories, but it's important to drink a glass of water with your wheat bran, as well a glass of water after you've finished your wheat bran-enriched meal.

Cereals — Grams of fiber

(based on 1/2 cup unless otherwise specified)

	Grams of fiber
Fiber First	15.0
Fiber One	12.8
All Bran	10.0
Oatmeal (1 cup)	5.0
Raisin Bran (3/4 cup)	4.6
Bran Flakes (1 cup)	4.4
Shreddies (2/3 cup)	2.7
Cheerios (1 cup)	2.2
Corn Flakes (1 1/4 cup)	0.8
Special K (1 1/4 cup)	0.4
Rice Krispies (1 1/4 cup)	0.3

Breads — Grams of fiber

(based on 1 slice)

	Grams of fiber
Rye	2.0
Pumpernickel	2.0
12-grain	1.7
100-percent whole wheat	1.3
Raisin	1.0
Cracked-wheat	1.0
White	0

Keep in mind that some of the newer high-fiber breads on the market today have up to 7 grams of fiber per slice. This chart is based on what is normally found in typical grocery stores.

Fruits and Vegetables

Another easy way of boosting fiber content is to know how much fiber your fruits and vegetables pack per serving. All fruits, beans (legumes), and vegetables listed here show measurements for insoluble fiber, which is not only good for colon health, but for your heart. Some of these numbers may surprise you!

Fruit — Grams of fiber

Fruit	Grams of fiber
Raspberries (3/4 cup)	6.4
Strawberries (1 cup)	4.0
Blackberries (1/2 cup)	3.9
Orange (1)	3.0
Apple (1)	2.0
Pear (1/2 medium)	2.0
Grapefruit (1/2 cup)	1.1
Kiwi (1)	1.0

Beans — Grams of fiber

(based on 1/2 cup unless otherwise specified)

Beans	Grams of fiber
Green beans (1 cup)	4.0
White beans	3.6
Kidney beans	3.3
Pinto beans	3.3
Lima beans	3.2

Vegetables — Grams of fiber

(based on 1/2 cup unless otherwise specified)

Vegetables	Grams of fiber
Baked potato with skin (1 large)	4.0
Acorn squash	3.8
Peas	3.0
Creamed, canned corn	2.7
Brussels sprouts	2.3
Asparagus (3/4 cup)	2.3
Corn kernels	2.1
Zucchini	1.4
Carrots (cooked)	1.2
Broccoli	1.1

Drink water with fiber

You probably know many people who say, "...but I *do* eat tons of fiber and I'm still constipated!" Probably quite a few. Well the reason they remain constipated in spite of their high-fiber diet is because they are not drinking *water* with fiber. Water means *water*. Milk, coffee, tea, soft drinks, or juice is not a substitute for water. Unless you drink water with your fiber, the fiber will not "bulk up" in your colon to create the nice, soft bowel movements you so desire. Think of fiber as a sponge. Obviously, a dry sponge won't work. You must soak it with water in order for it to be useful. Same thing here. Fiber without water is as useful as a dry sponge. *You gotta soak your fiber!* So here is the fiber/water recipe:

> ➤ **Drink two glasses of water with your fiber.** This means having a glass of water with whatever you're eating. Even if what you're eating does not contain much fiber, drinking water with your meal is a good habit to get into!

> ➤ **Drink two glasses of water after you eat.**

There are, of course, other reasons to drink lots of water throughout the day. For example, some studies show that dehydration can lead to mood swings and depression. Women are often advised from numerous health and beauty experts to drink eight to 10 glasses of water per day for other reasons; water helps you to lose weight; have well-hydrated, beautiful skin; and urinate regularly, which is important for bladder form and function (women, in particular, can suffer from bladder infections and urinary incontinence). By drinking water with your fiber, you'll be able to get up to that "eight glasses of water per day" in no time.

Vitamins Good for the Gut

It's believed that fruits and vegetables high in antioxidants, phytoestrogens (plant estrogens, found in soy, discussed in Chapter 1), and lignins may also protect against a variety of cancers. Vitamin A and beta-carotene are associated with preventing or even reversing lung, larynx, colon, prostate, bladder, stomach, esophageal, and possibly breast cancer. Vitamins C, and E and selenium are associated with low rates of stomach and esophageal cancers, in particular. It's believed that vitamins C and E block the formation of carcinogenic compounds in the stomach, including polyps. Vitamin D, which the body naturally makes when exposed to natural light, and calcium have been shown in some studies to protect against colorectal and breast cancers. Calcium apparently helps to absorb fecal bile acids, which experts believe promote tumors in the digestive tract. In fact, epidemiological studies show a higher incidence of colon and breast cancers in regions with less sunlight. (Although this could simply mean that where there's less sunlight, there's more sedentary living.) And finally, epidemiological studies suggest folic acid could lower the risk of colon cancer.

Herbs to keep you regular

You may have heard of acidophilus (liquid or powder) as a remedy for chronic constipation, which does not create a dependency. Or, in Ayervedic medicine (an ancient Indian healing system), *triphala* is taken to promote regularity and good digestion. Triphala is a combination of three ancient Ayurvedic ingredients: haritaki, bibhitaki, and amalaki. It can be found in most health food stores. In addition, the following spices are good for digestion, and are not harmful to your colon in any way: licorice root, peppermint leaf, anise seed, yellow dock root, dandelion root, coriander seed, celery seed, cinnamon bark, ginger root, cardamom seed, clove bud, and black pepper.

How to Move

Following a "heart-smart" exercise program is good for the gut, too. When oxygen flow is improved throughout your body, everything—including your digestive system—works better. There are also stretches you can do to help strengthen your abdominal muscles, which can help to combat constipation:

1. **The Squat.** By doing this regularly, you can become more regular, too! You simply stand with your feet parallel to your hips and slowly squat down, making sure your weight is forward (rather than reeling backward or rolling your knees inward). You may need to practice a few times before you can do this comfortably. Do this five times. It's recommended that you "squat" twice a day to aid with constipation.

2. **Knee-To-Chest (one leg).** This strengthens your abdominal muscles and, when combined with The Squat, can beautifully relieve chronic constipation. Lie on your back on the floor. Bend one knee and bring it in to the chest. Then just hug the leg, and slowly bring it toward your abdomen. Hold for a count of 10. Relax and repeat with alternate leg.

3. **Knee-To-Chest (both legs).** This is the same as the One Leg version, only you will bring both legs to the chest and hug them with both arms, bringing them gently toward your abdomen. Hold them there for the count of 10. Then relax and repeat.

Bone Health

Maintaining bone mass and good bone health is your best defense against bone loss, also known as osteoporosis. Eighty percent of all osteoporosis sufferers are women as a direct result of estrogen loss. Although osteoporosis can be disfiguring, it is a relatively "silent" disease because there are often no immediate symptoms, pain, or suffering that occur with it. The problem is not osteoporosis *per se*, but the risk of fractures. One out of two women over age 50 will have an osteoporosis-related fracture in her lifetime. If you have osteoporosis and fall down, a fracture can dramatically affect the quality of life you currently enjoy and can continue to enjoy for years to come. If you've ever experienced reduced mobility, or being dependent on someone else to prepare meals, shop, or run errands, you may have some idea as to how debilitating being bed-ridden and immobile can be. A full 70 percent of all hip fractures are a direct result of osteoporosis. Twenty percent of those suffering hip fractures will die; 50 percent will be disabled. In fact, more women die each year as a result of osteoporosis-related fractures than from breast and ovarian cancers combined.

The costs of osteoporosis are taking a toll on our healthcare system, too. This chapter explains what osteoporosis is and the dangers of fractures and discusses prevention strategies and therapy. What to Eat offers important information on diet, herbs, and supplements, and How to Move suggests a number of weight-bearing activities that can help to build bone mass.

What Is Osteoporosis?

Osteoporosis literally means "porous bones" and is perhaps the most feared condition in the postmenopausal community. Unfortunately, osteoporosis is not always preventable, and is a classic symptom of aging. Normally, in the life of a healthy, unremarkable woman, by her late 30s and 40s her bones become less dense. By the time she reaches her 50s, she may begin to experience bone loss in her teeth and become more susceptible to wrist fractures. Gradually, the bones in her spine weaken, fracture, and compress, causing upper back curvature and loss of height, known as kyphosis, or sometimes, "dowager's hump." If you've ever been stopped at a traffic light to watch an elderly woman stooped over, and struggling to get across the street in time, you've seen osteoporosis in full flare. You don't have to become such a sight; there are many ways to maintain bone mass after menopause and prevent the disfiguring effects of bone loss.

Why Women?

Osteoporosis is unfortunately more common in women because, when her skeletal growth is completed, she typically has 15 percent lower bone mineral density and 30 percent less bone mass than a man of the same age. Studies also show that women lose more trabecular bone (the inner, spongy part making up the internal support of the bone) at a higher rate than men.

There are three types of osteoporosis women are prone to: *postmenopausal, senile,* and *secondary. Postmenopausal osteoporosis* usually develops roughly 10 to 15 years after the onset of menopause. In this case, estrogen loss interferes with calcium absorption, and you begin to lose what's known as your *trabecular bone* three times faster than the normal rate of trabecular bone loss. You will also begin to lose parts of your *cortical bone* (the outer shell of the bone) but not as quickly as the trabecular bone.

Senile osteoporosis affects men and women. Here, you lose cortical and trabecular bone because of a decrease in bone cell activity that results from aging. Hip fractures are seen most often with this kind of osteoporosis. The decreased bone cell activity affects your capacity to rebuild bone in the first place, but it is also aggravated by low calcium intake.

Secondary osteoporosis means that there is an underlying condition that has caused bone loss. These conditions include chronic renal disease, hypogonadism (an overstimulation of the sex glands—gonads), hyperthyroidism (an overactive thyroid gland), some forms of cancer, gastrectomy (removal of parts of the intestine which interfere with calcium absorption), and the use of anticonvulsants.

Calcium

Your thyroid gland rents space to cells called C cells, which make the hormone calcitonin. This hormone helps to regulate calcium and helps to prevent osteoporosis. It is also used to treat Paget's disease, a bone disease that affects mostly men. But to your *bones*, calcitonin is kind of like a "tonsil": It serves a useful purpose, but when the hormone is not manufactured due to the absence of a thyroid gland (if it's removed or ablated because you've been treated for an overactive thyroid gland), you won't really notice any effects, just as you don't "miss" your tonsils. Calcium levels are really controlled by the parathyroid glands.

Everyone has at least four parathyroid glands that control the blood calcium level, or calcium balance. (Some people have more than four.) Your parathyroid glands stimulate the release of calcium from the bone to raise blood calcium levels. They also help your body convert vitamin D into calcium.

These glands are located on the back of each lobe of your thyroid gland. The easiest way to grasp exactly where they're located is to imagine the capital letter "H." At each tip of the "H," imagine a circle. If the "H" is your thyroid gland, the circles at each tip are your parathyroid glands.

What Causes Bone Loss, Anyway?

Our bones are always regenerating (known as "remodeling"). This process helps to maintain a constant level of calcium in the blood, essential for a healthy heart, blood circulation, and blood clotting. About 99 percent of all the body's calcium is in the bones and teeth; when blood calcium drops below a certain level, the body will *take* calcium from the bones to replenish it. But by the time we reach our late 30s, our bones lose calcium faster than it can be replaced. The pace of bone calcium loss speeds up for "freshly post-menopausal" women who are three to seven years beyond menopause. But bones start absorbing calcium again when this "bone-pause" is past. And consumption of calcium-rich plants, combined with moderate exercise, can help to reverse osteoporosis.

The pace then slows once again, but as we age the body is less able to absorb calcium from food. One of the most influential factors on bone loss is estrogen; it slows or even halts the loss of bone mass by improving our absorption of calcium from the intestinal tract, which allows us to maintain a higher level of calcium in our blood. The higher the calcium levels in the blood, the lower chance you have of losing calcium from your bones to replenish your calcium blood levels. In men, testosterone does the same thing for them regarding calcium absorption, but, unlike women, men never reach a particular age when their testes *stop* producing testosterone. If they did, they would be just as prone to osteoporosis as women.

There is a long list of other factors that affect bone loss. One of the most obvious factors is calcium in our diet. Calcium is regularly lost to urine, feces, and dead skin. We need to continuously account for this loss in our diet. In fact, the more infrequently we ingest calcium, the more we force our body into taking it out of our bones. Exercise also greatly affects bone density; the more we exercise, the stronger we make our bones. In fact the bone mass we have in our late 20s and early 30s will affect our bone mass at menopause.

Finally, there are several physical conditions and external factors that help to weaken our bones, contributing to bone loss later in life. These include:

- ➤ **Heavy caffeine and alcohol intake.** As diuretics, they cause you to lose more calcium in your urine. Heavy drinkers tend to suffer from more hip fractures. Because alcohol can damage the liver, which could impair its ability to metabolize vitamin D, it can aggravate bone loss.

- ➤ **Smoking.** Research shows that smokers tend to go into earlier menopause, and older smokers have 20–30 percent less bone mass than nonsmokers. Several studies have shown that women who smoke have a greater risk of fractures than women who do not.

- ➤ **Women in surgical menopause who are not on ERT** lose estrogen earlier than they would have naturally increases bone loss.

- ➤ **Antacids with aluminum and corticosteriods.**

- ➤ **Diseases of the small intestine, liver, and pancreas**. These prevent the body from absorbing adequate amounts of calcium from the intestine.

- ➤ **Lymphoma, leukemia, and multiple myeloma.**

- ➤ **Chronic diarrhea from ulcerative colitis or Crohn's disease.** This causes calcium loss through feces.

➤ **Surgical removal of part of the stomach or small intestine.** This affects absorption.

➤ **Hypercalciuria.** This is a condition where one loses too much calcium in the urine.

➤ **Early menopause** (before age 45). The earlier you stop producing estrogen, the more likely you are to lose calcium.

➤ **Lighter complexions.** Women with darker pigments have roughly 10 percent more bone mass than fairer women because they produce more *calcitonin*, the hormone that strengthens bones.

➤ **Low weight.** Women with less body fat store less estrogen, which makes the bones less dense to begin with and more vulnerable to calcium loss.

➤ **Women with eating disorders** (yo-yo dieting, starvation diets, binge/purge eaters). When there isn't enough calcium in bloodstream through our diet, the body will go to the bones to get what it needs. These women also have lower weight.

➤ **A family history of osteoporosis.** Studies show that women born to mothers with spinal fractures have lower bone mineral density in the spine, neck, and mid shaft.

➤ **High-protein diet.** This contributes to a loss of calcium in urine.

➤ **Women who have *never* been pregnant.** These women haven't experience the same bursts of estrogen in their bodies as women who *have* been pregnant.

➤ **Antacids with aluminum.** They interfere with calcium absorption.

➤ **Lactose intolerance.** Because so much calcium is found in dairy foods, this allergy is a significant risk factor.

➤ **Scoliosis.**

➤ **Women who had teenage pregnancy.** When a woman is pregnant in her teens, her bones are not yet fully developed and she can lose as much as 10 percent of her bone mass unless she has an adequate calcium intake of roughly 2000 mg during the pregnancy and 2,200 while breastfeeding.

Thyroid disease and osteoporosis

Women who suffer from an overactive thyroid gland, may be at greater risk of bone loss. That's because thyroid hormone will "speed up" or "slow down" bone cells just as it will speed or slow other parts of our bodies, such as our metabolism. Osteoblasts are the cells responsible for building bone; osteoclasts are cells that remove old bone so the new bone can be replaced. When you have an overactive thyroid gland (called hyperthyroidism), osteoclasts get overstimulated; in short, they go nuts. They begin to remove bone faster than it can be replaced by the osteoblasts, which are not affected by hyperthyroidism. So, you wind up with too much bone removed and bone loss. However, once your hyperthyroidism is treated and your thyroid hormone replacement medication is balanced, the risk is gone.

If Your Posture Is Affected

Women already affected by bone loss and may suffer from a slightly curved or disfigured posture, which can make clothing hang funny. The following are fashion and design tips from the National Osteoporosis Foundation (United States) in partnership with New York's Fashion Institute of Technology:

➤ Wear clothing that is loose, straight, or just slightly fitted.

➤ Jeweled, rounded, slight V, or soft cowl necklines work best.

> ➤ Choose raglan, dropped, or dolman sleeves.

> ➤ Find pants with elasticized waistbands.

> ➤ Wear dresses with empire waist, dropped waist or A-line.

> ➤ Make good use of accessories, such as long scarves or shawls to highlight the face and draw eyes up away from shoulder area.

> ➤ Add shoulder pads to compensate for sloping shoulders.

> ➤ Use backpacks to evenly distribute weight and leave hands free for balance.

> ➤ Wear flat or low-heeled comfortable slip-on shoes with rubber soles.

> ➤ Work with department store personal shoppers; they are usually free of charge.

> *Source: National Osteoporosis Foundation, 1999.*

Staying Hip About Fractures

One in four women over age 50 have osteoporosis, and as the 60s generation begins turning 50 in record numbers, we'll be facing a "fractured generation" of sorts—the most debilitating of which are hip fractures. Your risk of a hip fracture is equal to your combined risk of breast, uterine, and ovarian cancers.

In general, all bones are vulnerable to fractures, including the ribs, ankles, and pelvis. Osteoporosis-related fractures are categorized as wrist fractures, vertebral fractures, and, the most serious of all, hip fractures (a.k.a. fractures of the proximal femur).

Wrist fractures

Wrist fractures start to occur in women age 50 and older, and the incidence rises until age 65, and then sort of flattens out. You break your wrist usually by trying to break a fall. (Live in icy areas?) These heal fairly easily and don't lead to serious disability in the same way as hip fractures. But your wrist will still be stiff or sore, and, if you use a computer or work with your hands, it will obviously cause discomfort and lost time.

Vertebral fractures

These fractures are common within the first 20 postmenopausal years. This means if your last period was at 53, you can be vulnerable to these fractures until well into your 70s. This is when you may fall on the ice and fracture your tailbone. Women with bone loss in the teeth, or who have already suffered from wrist fractures, which contains trabecular bone, are most at risk for vertebral fractures.

Hip fractures

North American women have the highest rates of hip fractures. At 55, you have a 17-percent chance of sustaining a hip fracture, which compares to only 6 percent in men of the same age. And women are four times more likely to have a second hip fracture than women without a history of fractures. Why are hip fractures so serious? Currently, about 25 percent of people with hip fractures die from complications, such as pneumonia. The problem begins with being bed-ridden. You're lying in bed, in pain, on a lot of pain medications. You just get sicker and sicker until one thing leads to another—actually the fate of many long-term, chronic illness sufferers. Fifteen to 25 percent are still in long-term care institutions a year after the injury.

Most hip fractures occur in Caucasian or Asian women who are in their 70s and 80s. White women 65 or older have twice the incidence of fractures as African American women. But by "boning up" on calcium now (see "What to Eat"), you can help to prevent this very debilitating fate. Researchers aren't sure whether the high rate of hip fractures in the 70- and 80-year olds is due to poor nutrition in younger years. The difference between you and your mother is huge from a nutritional standpoint. Mom grew up during the Depression; you grew up during abundant times: in the 1950s. That said, your mother probably wasn't much of a dieter. Anyone coming of age in the Sixties was exposed to the Twiggy-like thinness, which has remained in vogue (and in *Vogue*) ever since. And, your mother may not have smoked and may not—ultimately—have been as sedentary as you may be. So the fracture statistics may "stick" for other reasons.

8 ways to avoid a fall

If you have suffered some bone loss, here are some tips to "fall-proof" your home:

1. Don't leave loose wires, cords, or slippery throw rugs lying around.

2. Make sure you have a non-slip mat in the shower or bathtub.

3. Install nightlights to avoid tripping in the middle of the night.

4. Clean up spills on the floors to avoid slipping.

5. Install treads, rails, or rugs on wooden stairs.

6. Start wearing comfortable, sturdy shoes with rubber soles.

7. Avoid activity when taking medications that can make you drowsy.

8. Cut down on alcohol. You can become clutsy and fall more easily when you're under the influence of alcohol.

Risky movements

If you have more severe bone loss, everyday movements can cause fractures. Watch out for the following:

> **Lifting heavy objects** (such as groceries) or excessive bending.

> **Forceful sneezing or coughing**.

> **Reaching above your shoulders** (as in reaching for something in closets or cupboards).

> **A sudden twist or turn,** which you may do when driving.

> **Getting in and out of beds or chairs.** Stiffness can be quite severe if you have osteoporosis; sitting or lying down in one position for too long can make the normal movements of getting up hazardous. Go slow. To lessen stiffness, use a pillow for back support, and avoid cold drafts.

Preventing Bone Loss

There are a few routes you can take to prevent bone loss. The ever-popular "diet and lifestyle changes" are the most natural route, and a route many women feel most comfortable with. Hormone Replacement Therapy is the second route. There are also a few osteoporosis-prevention drugs. The most recently approved drug is *raloxifene* (Evista), which came to market in 1998 and was developed by Eli Lilly (discussed under "OsteoDrugs"). You cannot combine HRT with Evista, however. You have to choose. But whichever you choose, you should combine a high-calcium diet and exercise with that therapy.

Neither HRT or Evista can guarantee freedom from fracture, because the bones may still be rigid rather than flexible. Only calcium and exercise can build flexible bone mass. For example, there are many women who faithfully take estrogen replacement therapy who still suffer fractures. That said, when estrogen replacement therapy is started at menopause, and continued for the rest of your life, it can reduce the rate of fractures by 40 to 60 percent. Women who do not take estrogen, who exercise regularly, and who have a diet high in calcium, can reduce their rate of fractures by at least 50 percent, too.

But it's not enough to just take calcium supplements or eat high-calcium foods; you need to cut down on foods that have diuretic qualities to them: caffeine and alcohol. How much is "enough" calcium? According to the National Institutes of Health Consensus Panel on Osteoporosis, premenopausal women require roughly 1,000 mg of calcium a day; for perimenopausal or postmenopausal women already on HRT or ERT 1,000 mg, and for peri and postmenopausal women not taking estrogen, roughly 1,500 mg per day. For women who have already been diagnosed with osteoporosis, the Panel recommends 2,500 mg of calcium a day. Foods that are rich in calcium include all dairy products (an 8 oz glass of milk contains 300 mg calcium), fish, shellfish, oysters, shrimp, sardines, salmon, soybeans, tofu, broccoli, and dark green vegetables (except spinach, which contains oxalic acid, preventing calcium absorption). It's crucial to determine how much calcium you're getting in your diet *before* you start any calcium supplements; too much calcium can cause kidney stones in people who are risk for them. In addition, not all supplements have been tested for absorbency. Dr. Robert Heaney suggests, in his book *Calcium and Common Sense,* that you test absorbency yourself by dropping your supplement into a glass of warm water while stirring occasionally. If the supplement doesn't dissolve completely, chances are it won't be absorbed by your body efficiently. It's crucial to remember that a calcium supplement is in fact a supplement and should not replace a high-calcium diet. So the dosage of your supplement would only need to be the usual 400–600 mg per day, as your diet should account for the remainder of your 1000–1500 daily intake of calcium.

The most accurate way to measure your risk of osteoporosis is through a bone densitometry (or "DEXA"), which measures bone mass and provides you with a "fracture risk estimate." This test involves low-radiation X-rays and takes about 30 minutes.

Osteodoctors

Many women want to know who is an "osteoporosis specialist." Although primary care physicians (family physicians or general practitioners) can manage osteoporosis, if you want to consult with a specialist, there are a few you can see, but no single "osteoporosis specialist" per se. Endocrinologists may be one route, because this is a condition associated with estrogen-loss and sometimes calcium deficiencies. Rheumatologists, who manage joint pain, are also popular choices, as well as gerontologists, who specialize in aging and diseases of aging.

But more practical specialists for you may be physiotherapists, who can help you strengthen muscles and bones, and even occupational therapists, who can help you avoid injuries and get you custom splints or orthopedic "paraphernalia" to help you cope with a previous injury. Many find acupuncture helpful in dealing with joint pain as well.

OsteoDrugs

Although there are other drugs in development, as of this writing, there are four different drugs used in preventing and reversing osteoporosis. That said, the best prevention therapy is a high-calcium diet combined with exercise. None of the following drug therapies are designed to replace lifestyle changes, and you're encouraged to combine calcium diets and exercise with these therapies.

Hormone Replacement Therapy

By replacing estrogen, you can help to retard the bone-loss process, because it is estrogen that is crucial for calcium absorption in the first place. Not all women should be on estrogen, and many women do not want to take estrogen, which makes them good candidates for the next drug discussed. Studies also show that postmenopausal women who take two Tums per day can cut their dosage of daily estrogen in half; half the HRT dose and two Tums will prevent bone loss just as well as a full dose of HRT. This is a good option if your reasons for refusing HRT are because of fears of breast cancer risk (see Chapter 1). Women in this Tums study were given two 600-mg Tums-EXTRA tablets, a vitamin D supplement to aid calcium absorption by the body, and 0.3 mg of estrogen. The women on low-dosage estrogen showed as much as a 5.2-percent increase in bone-mass density, which is comparable to higher dose HRT regimens.

Selective Estrogen Receptor Modulators

Selective Estrogen Receptor Modulators (SERMs) are a new class of drugs originally designed to help treat estrogen-dependent breast cancers, but were instead shown to help prevent bone loss—particularly around the spine and hip—and even increase bone mass. The first drug from this family, approved for use in 1998, is raloxifene (Evista). Women who took raloxifene for three years reduced their risk of fractures by about 50 percent. Even better, raloxifene may help protect you from heart disease—good news if you are at risk for heart disease because it helps lower "bad cholesterol" (see Chapter 2). This is great news for women who cannot take HRT because of a history of breast cancer, for example. Some studies also suggest that raloxifene may also reduce the incidence of breast cancer in some women. Raloxifene and HRT are equally effective in protecting your bones. And of course, you can continue to take calcium and/or vitamin D with raloxifene.

The *bad news* is that there are some estrogen-like side effects, including hot flashes and the risk of blood clots. However, it doesn't cause breast tenderness or bloating. And unlike HRT, raloxifene does not help with the signs of menopause, and it may even aggravate them. You cannot take raloxifene unless you are postmenopausal, meaning that you have been free from periods for at least one year. The drug has not been tested in women still having periods. If you are taking warfarin or other coumarin blood thinners, you may also not be able to take this drug and should discuss it with your doctor.

Ideal raloxifene users are postmenopausal women at risk for osteoporosis and heart disease who are not taking HRT, or postmenopausal women at risk for osteoporosis and highrisk for breast cancer. Women who should take raloxifene include:

> **Premenopausal women.**

> **Pregnant women or women who are breastfeeding.**

> **Women with a history of blood clots or leg cramps** (signs of possible blood clots).

> **Women on any form of estrogen or progestin therapy** that comes as a pill, patch, or injection.

> **Women taking cholestyramine or colestipol.**

> **Women with liver problems.**

Bisphosphonates: bone-forming drugs

As discussed earlier, osteoblasts are the cells responsible for building bone, and osteoclasts are cells that remove old bone so the new bone can be replaced. Bisphosphonates stop or slow down the osteoclasts without interfering with osteoblasts, the bone-forming cells. So you wind up with greater bone density. In the past, these drugs were approved only for treating severe bone diseases, such as Paget's disease. Two bisphosphonates—etidronate (DIDROCAL/DIDRONEL) and alendronate (FOSAMAX)—have been approved for use in women who are not on HRT, but who are at risk of osteoporosis. However, bisphosphonates do not relieve any menopausal signs, such as hot flashes, and offers no protection against heart disease.

Bisphosphonates are equally effective in reducing the risk of fractures as HRT and raloxifene (the rate is reduced by about 50 percent in women taking the drug for about three years). If you're taking bisphosphanates, however, you **cannot** take calcium supplements *at the same time*, because calcium prevents the body from absorbing the bisphosphonate. If you're taking alendronate, you'll need to wait 30 minutes after taking it before you have food or take a calcium supplement. If you're taking etidronate, you'll need to take the drug in a cycle, which your doctor will discuss with you, so you can take calcium supplements. In general, alendronate is a more potent, more effective bisphosphonate. The side effects of etidronate and alendronate may include nausea, abdominal pain, or loose bowel movements. In rare instances, some people develop skin rashes or esophageal ulcers.

Calcitonin

The hormone calcitonin is sometimes used to slow bone loss in women who are at least five years beyond their menopause. But this is a much cruder way to prevent bone loss and can only be taken as an injection or spray, because it cannot be metabolized orally. And unlike the other previously mentioned drugs, it does not help in reducing fractures or *building* bone mass. Calcitonin is fast becoming the dinosaur in osteoporosis prevention, and there are no good reasons at this point in time to take calcitonin injections in light of much better therapies.

What to Eat

Calcium can be eaten. And there are many kinds of foods high in calcium. This is your best protection from bone loss, combined with weight bearing activities (see "How to Move").

Ways to Increase Calcium

Think of calcium as a retirement fund. You want to build up a reserve that your body can use when it ages. Your bones are the "savings account" where all excess calcium is deposited. When the savings account is full, you gain bone mass. When the savings account is depleted, you go into "calcium debt." When this happens, your parathyroid gland produces a hormone that triggers the release of calcium stores from the bone, and you lose bone mass. So in order to keep calcium in that savings account, you have to increase your calcium intake. That means eating three or more calcium-rich foods daily and avoiding foods that cause you to use up or "pee out" calcium, such as salt, coffee, meat, fluoride, soda, and white flour products.

Maximizing calcium absorption

Calcium is best absorbed in an acidic environment. To increase acidity:

> Drink lemon juice in water with or after your meal.

> Add two tablespoons/30 ml apple cider vinegar and two tablespoons raw honey or blackstrap molasses to a cup/250 ml water; drink with or after your meal.

> Use calcium-rich herbal vinegar in your salad dressing.

Calcium greens

> Broccoli, kale, turnip greens, or mustard greens contain about 200 mg calcium. One cup cooked collards, wild onions, lamb's quarter, or amaranth greens, about 400 mg calcium.

> The following greens are not high calcium sources, but high iron sources: spinach, swiss chard (silver beet), beet greens, wood sorrel, or rhubarb.

High-calcium sources

Some of these you probably know about; many of these you don't:

- ➤ Tahini.
- ➤ Soy or tofu (not all tofu contains calcium; check labels).
- ➤ Oats/oatmeal.
- ➤ Seaweed.
- ➤ Sardines.
- ➤ Yogurt.
- ➤ Nettles.
- ➤ Dandelion leaves.
- ➤ Dried fruit (65 mg of calcium in three small figs, a handful of raisins, four dates, or eight prunes).
- ➤ Corn tortillas. (Because these are made with lime, these are high in calcium.)

Calcium-rich herbs

A big mug of infusion using any of these herbs is equal to 250–300 mg calcium. Add a big pinch of horsetail and increase the calcium by 10 percent.

Nettle.	Sage.
Chickweed.	Red clover.
Comfrey leaf.	Raspberry leaf.
Oatstraw.	

Dairy products

The highest calcium dairy product is live-culture yogurt (from milk without hormone and antibiotic residues). Yogurt also strengthens the digestive system, boosts the immune system, eases the nervous system, and helps prevent vaginal infections. Yogurt is much lower in fat than other dairy products, in case you want to stay heart-healthy. In fact, 25 percent (350–400 mg) of your 1500 mg daily calcium requirement can come from 1 cup/250 ml yogurt, which is equal to 1 cup of milk, 1 ounce/30 grams hard cheese, or 1/2 cup/115 grams ricotta cheese. One cup of soy milk yields 80 mg calcium and 1 cup almond milk yields 165 mg calcium.

Calcium supplements

If you can't get enough calcium in your diet, there are always supplements: 500 mg magnesium (not citrate) with calcium. Better yet, wash your calcium pill down with a glass of herbal infusion; that will provide not only magnesium but lots of other synergistic minerals, too. Calcium supplements are more effective in divided doses. Two doses of 250 mg, taken morning and night, actually provide more usable calcium than a 1,000 mg tablet. New research also shows that the amount of calcium absorbed from calcium citrate supplements is consistently higher than the amount absorbed from calcium carbonate supplements. Popular supplements include:

➤ **Calcium-fortified orange juice.** This is easier to digest and absorb then other supplements.

➤ **Calcium citrate in tablet form** (crushed tablets are better absorbed).

➤ **Calcium gluconate, calcium lactate, and calcium carbonate** (if chewable). You can take 1,500 mg daily of one of these.

A sample high-calcium daily diet:

➤ 1 tsp./5 ml seaweed such as kelp.

➤ 2 cups/500ml fresh or 1 cup/250ml cooked dark greens.

➤ 1 cup yogurt or whey.

➤ A big mug of calcium-rich herbal infusion.

➤ 1 tbs. herbal vinegar.

➤ 1 tbs. lemon juice in which egg shell has soaked overnight.

➤ 2 tbs. blackstrap molasses.

Other Bone Supplements

➤ **Fruits and vegetables high in zinc, magnesium, potassium** (slows calcium excretion), fiber, and vitamin C (aids in bone formation) can keep bones strong and fracture free.

➤ **Wild yam cream**, which also contains a naturally derived progesterone.

➤ **Supplements of up to 50,000 units beta-carotene** daily increases progesterone production and protects bones.

➤ **Microcrystalline hydroxapatite** is specifically formulated to deposit minerals into the bones. Helps reverse osteoporosis and heal compression fractures in the spine.

➤ **Vitamin D supplements** (if you cannot spend 10–15 minutes in the sun daily). The recommended dose is 400–800 IU daily.

➤ **Horsetail herb** *(Equisetum arvense)*. Increases calcium absorption.

➤ **Dandelion root tincture.** Increases calcium absorption.

How to Move

As one fitness expert told me, "If you want a strong house, you need a strong frame." When you increase the load on your bones, your bones increase in mass; similarly, when you decrease the load on your bones, they decrease in mass. And the denser your bones, the harder they are to break or sprain. That's why exercises that build bone mass are important to combating osteoporosis. Carrying weights is one of the best ways to increase bone mass, and doing weight-bearing activities is also encouraged because it builds bone mass and uses up calories. By increasing muscular strength through these activities, we also increase flexibility (to help combat falls) and endurance. For example, you'll find that the first time you ride your bike from home to downtown, your legs may feel sore. Do that same ride 10 times, and your legs will no longer be sore. That's what's meant by building endurance. Of course, you won't be as out of breath, either, which is another way of building endurance.

Hand weights or resistance exercises (using rubber-band products or pushing certain body parts together) help increase what's called "lean body mass"—body tissue that is not fat. That is why many people find their weight does not drop when they begin to exercise. Leg lifts and arm lifts with weights increase balance, bone strength, and help maintain flexibility. Begin with one-pound weights and increase slowly to four to five pounds.

Other forms of resistance exercise involve moving objects or your own body weight to create resistance, using equipment at your gym or fitness center, or even using common household objects such as water jugs or canned goods. Wearing Velcro weights to your wrists and ankles and just moving around as you normally would are also good ways to increase resistance.

And as your muscles become bigger, and bones become denser, your body fat decreases. It's recommended that you do weight-bearing exercise four times a week for 30 minutes.

Enjoyable Activities
That May Help Build Bone Mass

Try to choose one activity from this list that is *your* enjoyable sport. If you enjoy your activity, you'll do it more often:

Walking.	Running.
Jogging.	Bicycling.
Hiking.	Tai chi.
Cross-country skiing.	Gardening.
Weight lifting.	Snow shoeing.
Climbing stairs.	Tennis.
Bowling.	Rowing.
Dancing.	Water workouts.
Badminton.	Basketball.
Volleyball.	Soccer.

Stretches and Postures

The following are not "weight-bearing" exercises (traditional exercises that build bone mass). Instead, these improve flexibility and help to stimulate acupressure points:

➤ Cobra (Upward Facing Dog): Lie on your belly with your palms down and adjacent to your shoulders. Slowly raise your upper body, lifting all but the lower abdomen toward the ceiling. Breathe deeply. Release.

➤ Sit on the floor with knees bent. Partially extend your right leg, holding the middle of the sole of the foot with the index and middle fingers of your right hand. Hold with steady pressure for one to three minutes. Breathe deeply. Repeat on your left side.

➤ Move your right hand to the point behind your ankle bone. Again, hold with steady pressure for one to three minutes. Repeat on the left side.

➤ Stand up and hold the point above your bladder, maintaining steady pressure for one to three minutes.

Natural Hormone Replacement Therapy

In light of what the studies reveal about conventional HRT, many of you may be interested in investigating natural hormone replacement therapy (NHRT), which includes natural progesterone. NHRT is a combination of human estrogens and natural human progesterone. HRT, on the other hand, is a "factory-made" estrogen, much of which is derived from horse estrogen and a factory-made progesterone called progestin. Now, many reports and studies show that the symptoms of menopause are better controlled with NHRT with fewer side effects. Studies also show that the protection from osteoporosis is more dramatic and pronounced using NHRT.

What NHRT Contains

When you go on NHRT, you're getting about 60–80 percent estriol, 10 to 20 percent estrone, and 10 to 20 percent estradiol, as well as: natural human progesterone and DHEA (dehydroepiandrosterone), a "natural androgen" if you will, which turns into a "natural testosterone" in the body, something all women need to maintain sex drives. On HRT, you're getting 75–80 percent estrone, 6–15 percent equilin, a horse-derived estrogen, and about 5–19 percent of estradiol, as well as progestin, a "factory-made" progesterone, as well as sometimes anabolic steroids if your libido needs a boost.

The bottom line is that human women do better with human hormones rather than animal-derived hormones, just like human infants do better on human milk than cow's milk. However, as you can see from the range of concentrations of various natural estrogens, it may take a while for you to find just the right "dose" of each kind of natural estrogen and progesterone, so you have to work with your doctor and experiment until you get it "right." There is a perception "out there" that NHRT is perfect the first time you take it, and many women have to tinker with their "triple estrogens" before they find the right combination for them. A typical prescription for NHRT is often 10 percent estrone, 10 percent estradiol and 80 percent estriol, mixed with about 25–30 mg of natural progesterone after menopause and 10–30 mg DHEA, which should, but doesn't always, convert into necessary amounts of testosterone. (If it doesn't, you may need to add a steroid to the mix of natural hormones if your libido is very low, which can be debilitating.)

Where do you find NHRT?

All the books and articles about the natural hormone therapy can mislead you into thinking that they are just available "everywhere." This is not so. You can't just walk into a health food store and buy natural estrogens or progesterones. They need to be prescribed by a doctor (although the doctor need not be an M.D.; several naturopathic doctors are prescribing them, too). A pharmacist has to prepare a doctor's prescription for NHRT from "scratch." This is known as a "compounding pharmacist." Not all pharmacies are "compounding pharmacies," so ask your doctor or current pharmacist about where to go to get a prescription prepared. You can also call the International Academy of Coumpounding Pharmacists (IACP) or the Professional Compunding Centers of America, Inc. (PCCA) for the nearest compounding pharmacist in your area. Most compounding pharmacists are members of either or both organizations. You can reach the PCCA at 800–331–2498 or at *www.compassnet.com/*

~ iacp/. Other compounding pharmacies include ApotheCure, based in Dallas, Texas, at (800) 969-6601 or online at *www.apothecure.com.* Women's International Pharmacy, based in Madison, Wisconsin can be reached at (800) 279–5708 or online at *www.womensinternational.com.* Although you must go to a compounding pharmacist to find natural progesterone, what you can get over the counter in some health food stores and natural pharmacies are creams containing botanical progesterone, which is progesterone that comes from plants such as wild yam. This is not harmful, but will not be as pure as the progesterone your doctor prescribes, which often comes from soy and wild yam, too, but is a very pure extraction. The term natural does not mean "human"; it means that it is not synthetic. Natural progesterone is recognized by our progesterone receptors as if it were progesterone we made in our bodies.

Creams

Natural progesterone works very well in cream form. There are few kinds:

➤ Creams that contain only progesterone in a carrier such as aloe vera or vitamin E.

➤ Creams with progesterone and other essential oils or herbs.

➤ Creams that contain progesterone and phytoestrogens (plant estrogens).

➤ Creams that contain progesterone and three kind of natural estrogen.

Creams that contain estrogen are ideally suited for menopausal women who are using natural hormone therapy to relieve estrogen loss and other menopausal discomforts.

Natural progesterone can also be found in an oil form (taken under the tongue), tablets, capsules, vaginal suppositories, vaginal gel, and in an injectable form.

Phytoestrogens

If you are uncomfortable with the idea of taking any kind of hormone replacement therapy, you may wish to consider the therapeutic benefits of phytoestrogens, or plant estrogens. Women are treating their discomforts with herbs (outlined in the What to Eat section in Chapter 1). Phytoestrogens contain a multitude of chemicals, including estrogenic substances. Although phytoestrogens have been used in Asian cultures for centuries to treat hot flashes, they're just beginning to catch on in the West. The first controlled trial began in 1996 at Columbia-Presbyterian Medical Center in New York.

Many food sources, such as tofu and soy, contain such high concentrations of phytoestrogens that scientists believe it may account for the incredible lack of menopausal discomforts in Japan, which has a soy-heavy diet. Blood levels of phytoestrogens are 10 to 40 times higher in Japanese women than in their Western counterparts, but Japanese women report hot flashes about 1/6 as often as Western women. Even the average vegetarian would not consume nearly as much soy as the average Japanese woman.

More interesting, plant hormones not only help prevent menopausal discomforts, but may protect you from breast cancer; breast cancer rates are dramatically lower in Japan than in the United States, but there may be other factors involved, such as childbearing habits and low fat. After menopause, high-fat diets can increase your risk of heart attack and stroke—no matter how much estrogen you take. Meanwhile, bad habits, such as coffee, alcohol, and smoking, can all increase your risk of osteoporosis. Right now, most doctors will tell you to go ahead and add as much soy as you want to your diet. It may well help, and it certainly can't hurt! Soy has most recently been declared a "heart-healthy" food.

What are the drawbacks?

The problem with phytoestrogens is that they are plant hormones, and not human hormones, which means that they will not solve the problem of rising FSH and LH levels (the gonadotropins, which "kick start" the ovaries). However, some plants do encourage estrogen production, and some do contain flavonoids, which are estrogen-like.

Plant hormones can be converted to human hormones in a laboratory. What plant hormones do is to provide you with hormonal building blocks rather than hormones themselves, which, in theory, can allow you to create the amounts (and combinations) of hormones you need for your unique menopausal journey.

It is possible to have allergic reactions to a variety of herbs. It's also important to note that, because herbal products are not regulated, there is a danger of misuse, overuse, or using poor quality merchandise.

Phytoestrogens can be taken orally or even in creams, which can be applied to your body parts. Creams are "quasi-natural," however, because the plant hormones they contain are modified in a lab. One good question many women are asking is whether phytoestrogens carry the same risks as HRT. The answer is that, because plant-based hormones contain chemicals that are similar but not identical to your natural estrogen, the risks of plant hormones are that you may still suffer from discomfort associated with estrogen loss in spite of your dedication to ingesting plant hormones.

The Estrogen Dominance Theory

Dr. John Lee is the next big name in the natural progesterone story. In the mid-1990s he began to publish his theory that that many women are progesterone-deficient due to estrogen dominance that can be caused by synthetic estrogens in oral contraceptives or other hormone therapies; obesity, which results in too much estrogen because fat cells make estrogen; and estrogen pollution, caused by the flushed urine of women on all these synthetic estrogens, which gets into our sewage systems and water supply, as well as another form of pollution known as environmental estrogens, also called xenoestrogens, which are beyond our control. Hormones in meat are other sources of estrogen. Estrogen dominance can cause a myriad of women's health problems. Unless there is an equal ratio of progesterone to estrogen, estrogen dominance can mean a progesterone deficiency. And for some women, that translates into more severe menopausal symptoms. The following tables will help you determine whether estrogen and progesterone are in balance.

Table 6.1
Signs of Estrogen Dominance

Accelerated aging.	Dry eyes.	Irregular cycles.
Allergies (asthma, rashes, sinus congestion).	Early menstruation.	Irritability.
	Fatigue.	Memory loss.
Autoimmune disorders.	Fibrocystic breasts.	Miscarriage.
		Mood swings.
Blood clots and risk of stroke.	Fibroids.	Osteoporosis prior to menopause.
	Gallbladder disease.	
Breast tenderness.		PMS.
Cervical dysplasia.	Hair loss.	Slow metabolism.
Decreased libido.	Headaches.	
Depression, anxiety, and agitation.	Hypoglycemia.	Uterine cancer.
	Hypothyroidism.	Water retention/ bloating.
Difficulty concentrating.	Infertility.	
	Insomina.	Weight gain.

Source: Rushton A., and Dr. Shirley Bond: *Natural Progesterone* (1999:6).

Table 6.2
What Estrogen Is Normally Supposed to Do to the Body

This list isn't exhaustive, but here are some major actions of estrogen:

➤ Decreases libido.

➤ Impairs blood sugar control (counterbalanced by progesterone).

➤ Increases blood clotting (counterbalanced by progesterone).

➤ Increases body fat (counterbalanced by progesterone).

➤ Interferes with thyroid hormone (counterbalanced by progesterone).

➤ Reduces oxygen levels in cells (counterbalanced by progesterone).

➤ Reduces vascular tone.

➤ Retains salt and fluids.

➤ Slows bone loss (counterbalanced by progesterone).

➤ Stimulates breasts (counterbalanced by progesterone).

➤ Thickens the lining of the uterus (counterbalanced by progesterone).

Note: When not counterbalanced by progesterone, many of these normal functions can turn into diseases, such as breast cancer or uterine cancer.

Source: Rushton A., and Dr. Shirley Bond: *Natural Progesterone* (1999:4).

Table 6.3
What Progesterone Is Normally Supposed to Do to the Body

This list isn't exhaustive, but here are some major actions of progesterone:

➤ Maintains the uterine lining with secretions.

➤ Counterbalances breast stimulation.

➤ Helps convert fat into energy.

➤ Is a natural diuretic.

➤ Is a natural anti-depressant.

➤ Facilitates thyroid hormone (counterbalanced by estrogen).

➤ Normalizes blood sugar levels (counterbalanced by estrogen).

➤ Normalizes blood clotting.

➤ Increases libido.

➤ Normalizes zinc and copper levels.

➤ Restores cell oxygen levels.

➤ Stimulates bone-building cells.

Note: When it's balanced, progesterone helps protect against many diseases, such as breast cancer or uterine cancer.

Source: Rushton A., and Dr. Shirley Bond: *Natural Progesterone* (1999:4).

Herbs for Perimenopause

Black Cohosh *(Cimicifuga racemosa)*, Schwarze Sclangenwurzel
(Chinese herbalists use Sheng Ma: C. foetida, C. dahurica)

Medicinal effects:

- ➤ Reduces intensity and frequency of hot flashes.
- ➤ Eases the general discomforts of menopause.
- ➤ Tones and strengthens pelvic floor muscles, preventing and correcting uterine and bladder prolapses.
- ➤ Improves digestion.
- ➤ Relieves menstrual pain and irregularity.
- ➤ Relieves headaches.
- ➤ Relieves angina pain and thins the blood.
- ➤ Calms the nerves.
- ➤ Alleviates water retention and breast tenderness.
- ➤ Aids with incontinence.

Vitex or Chaste Tree *(Vitex agnus-castii)*
(Chinese herbalists use Man Jing Zi)

➤ Helps improve endometriosis and uterine fibroids.

➤ Reduces severity of hot flashes.

➤ Relieves chronic menstrual cramps.

➤ Relieves heavy bleeding and spotting and irregular cycles.

➤ Calms the nerves.

➤ Clears up skin problems.

➤ Relieves hormone-related constipation and digestive.

➤ Lessens breast tenderness.

➤ Relieves water retention.

➤ Relieves PMS.

➤ Protects against reproductive cancers.

➤ Protects against osteoporosis.

Liferoot *(Senecio aureus)*/ Groundsel *(Senecio vulgaris)*/ Jacob's Groundsel *(Snecio jacobaea)*

➤ Relieves severe menstrual pain.

➤ Alleviates hot flashes.

➤ Tones uterus.

➤ Regulates the menstrual cycle.

➤ Calms the nerves.

➤ Relieve PMS symptoms and breast tenderness.

➤ Reduces urinary tract problems.

➤ Increases libido.

Garden sage *(Salvia officinalis)*, Salbei, Sauge officinale
Do not use: sagebrush/desert sage (Artemisia tridentata)

➤ Relieves night sweats, cold sweats, and hot flash sweats.

➤ Calms the nerves.

➤ Relieves dizziness, trembling, and mood swings associated with profuse sweating.

➤ Relives headaches.

➤ Strengthens the liver and aids digestion.

➤ Relieves menstrual cramps and heavy bleeding.

➤ Reduces bladder infections.

➤ Prevents joint aches, and increases circulation.

➤ Improves mental clarity and memory.

Motherwort *(Leonurus cardiaca)*, Herzgespan, Yi Mu Cao

➤ Lessens the severity, frequency, and duration of hot flashes.

➤ Relieves faintness associated with hot flashes.

➤ Calms the nerves, and helps lift depression.

➤ Relieves insomnia and sleep disturbances.

➤ Strengthens the heart, and reduces palpitations and tachycardia.

➤ Relieves menstrual cramps or uterine cramps.

➤ Restores thickness and elasticity to vaginal walls.

➤ Reduces water retention.

➤ Relieves constipation, and improves digestion.

Ginseng
Oriental Ginseng/Ren Shan (Panax ginseng)
American Ginseng *(Panax quinquefolius)*
Note: American ginseng is less potent than the ginseng grown in Korea and China.

➤ Reduces the intensity and frequency of hot flashes.

➤ Calms the nerves and lifts.

➤ Reduces stress.

➢ Improves overall energy levels, and reduces fatigue.

➢ Improves memory, concentration, mental acuity, and clarity.

➢ Normalizes blood pressure, and reduces cholesterol.

➢ Stabilizes blood sugar swings.

➢ Reduces headaches associated with menopause.

➢ Improves digestion.

➢ Enhances libido.

Dang Gui *(Angelic sinensis)* or *Dong Quai*

➢ Relieves hot flashes.

➢ Regulates the menstrual cycle. (*Note: If you have unpredictable episodes of heavy menstrual bleeding it may aggravate the problem.*)

➢ Relieves uterine cramps.

➢ Helps reduce vaginal dryness and thinning.

➢ Helps restore complexion.

➢ Reduces headaches and water retention.

➢ Reduces blood pressure, and improves circulation (contains coumarins, such as aspirin).

➢ Reduces insomnia.

➢ Calms the nerves.

➢ Relieves menopausal rheumatism.

➢ Tones the liver.

Note: Do not use Dang Gui if you have heavy bleeding, fibroids, diarrhea, or edema, or if you regularly take aspirin or other blood-thinning drugs.

Herbs for Postmenopause

Horsetail *(Equisetum arvense)*
- ➤ Reverses osteoporosis.
- ➤ Stimulates fracture-mending and bone repair.
- ➤ Stabilizes and reverses gum disease and loss of jaw bone.
- ➤ Relieves cystitis (bladder infection).
- ➤ Reduces bloat.
- ➤ Improves circulation.
- ➤ Increases energy, reduces fatigue.
- ➤ Nourishes hair and fingernails.

Oatstraw (*Avena sativa*; from the same oats you eat for breakfast)
- ➤ Helps build bones.
- ➤ Maintains teeth.
- ➤ Stabilizes blood sugar levels.
- ➤ Relieves depression.
- ➤ Reduces cholesterol.
- ➤ Maintains restful sleep patterns.
- ➤ Helps with bladder spasms, incontinence, uterine pain, and vaginal dryness.

Seaweeds
- Helps prevent osteoporosis.
- Lowers blood pressure and cholesterol.
- Helps with varicose veins and hemorrhoids.
- Nourishes the heart.
- Relieves incontinence, vaginal dryness, and persistent hot flashes.
- Increases immunity.
- Increases stamina.
- Minimize the effects of stress, chemicals, and radiation.
- Improves digestion.
- Restores libido.
- Eases sore joints.
- Nourishes skin and hair.

Stinging Nettle *(Urtica doica, Urtica urens)*
- Nourishes kidneys and adrenal glands.
- Relieves bladder infections, bloat, and incontinence.
- Rehydrates dry vaginal tissues.
- Helps maintain.
- Stabilizes blood sugar.
- Reduces headaches.
- Improves immunity.
- Improves digestion.
- Strengthens nervous system.
- Nourishes cardiovascular system.
- Nourishes skin and hair.

Bioflavonoids
All foods and herbs rich in bioflavonoids will help:
- Restore vaginal lubrication.
- Improve pelvic tone.
- Strengthen the bladder.
- Reduce water retention.
- Ease sore joints.
- Improve hot flashes.
- Improve liver activity.
- Lower risk of stroke and heart attack.
- Reduce muscle cramping.
- Improve resistance to infection.

Foods and herbs rich in bioflavonoids include:
- Citrus fruits.
- Buckwheat greens, such as alfalfa sprouts.
- Elder.
- Hawthorn.
- Knotweeds, Ho Shou Wu.
- Shepherd's purse.
- Sea buckhorn.
- Toadflax.
- White dead nettle.

Vitamins and Minerals for Fiftysomething

Vitamin A/Beta-Carotene: Found in liver, fish oils, egg yolks, whole milk, butter; Beta Carotene: leafy greens, yellow and orange vegetables and fruits. Depleted by: coffee, alcohol, cortisone, mineral oil, fluorescent lights, liver "cleansing," excessive intake of iron, lack of protein.

Vitamin B$_6$: Found in meats, poultry, fish, nuts, liver, bananas, avocados, grapes, pears, egg yolk, whole grains, legumes. (See vitamin B12 for depletions.)

Vitamin B$_{12}$: Found in meats, dairy products, eggs, liver, fish. Both B12 and B6 depleted by: coffee, alcohol, tobacco, sugar, raw oysters, birth control pills.

Vitamin C: Found in citrus fruits, broccoli, green pepper, strawberries, cabbage, tomato, cantaloupe, potatoes, leafy greens. Herbal sources: rose hips, yellow dock root, raspberry leaf, red clover, hops, nettles, pine needles, dandelion greens, alfalfa, echinacea, skullcap, parsley, cayenne, and paprika. Depleted by: antibiotics, aspirin, and other pain relievers, coffee, stress, aging, smoking, baking soda, and high fever.

Vitamin D: Found in fortified milk, butter, leafy green vegetables, egg yolk, fish oils, butter, liver, skin exposure to sunlight, shrimp. Herbal sources: none; not found in plants. Depleted by: mineral oil used on the skin, frequent baths, sunscreens with SPF 8 or more.

Vitamin E: Found in nuts, seeds, whole grains, fish-liver oils, freshly leafy greens, kale, cabbage asparagus. Herbal sources: alfalfa, rose hips, nettles, Dang Gui, watercress, dandelions, seaweeds, wild seeds. Depleted by: mineral oil, sulphates.

Vitamin K: Found in leafy greens, corn and soybean oils, liver, cereals, dairy products, meats, fruits, egg yolk, blackstrap molasses. Herbal sources: nettles, alfalfa, kelp, green tea. Depleted by: X-rays, radiation, air pollution, enemas, frozen foods, antibiotics, rancid fats, aspirin.

Thiamine (vitamin B1): Found in asparagus, cauliflower, cabbage, kale, spirulina, seaweeds, citrus. Herbal sources: peppermint, burdock, sage, yellow dock, alfalfa, red clover, fenugreek, raspberry leaves, nettles, catnip, watercress, yarrow, rose hips.

Riboflavin (B2): Found in beans, greens, onions, seaweeds, spirulina, dairy products, mushrooms. Herbal sources: peppermint, alfalfa, parsley, echinacea, yellow dock, hops, dandelion, ginseng, dulse, kelp, fenugreek.

Pyridoxine (B6): Found in baked potato with skin, broccoli, prunes, bananas, dried beans and lentils, all meats, poultry, fish.

Folic acid (B factor): Found in liver, eggs, leafy greens, yeast, legumes, whole grains, nuts, fruits (bananas, orange juice, grapefruit juice), vegetables (broccoli, spinach, asparagus, brussels sprouts). Herbal sources: nettles, alfalfa, parsley, sage, catnip, peppermint, plantain, comfrey leaves, chickweed.

Niacin (B factor): Found in grains, meats, and nuts, and especially: asparagus, spirulina, cabbage, bee pollen. Herbal sources: hops, raspberry leaf, red clover, slippery elm, echinacea, licorice, rose hips, nettles, alfalfa, parsley.

Bioflavonoids: Found in citrus pulp and rind. Herbal sources: buckwheat greens, blue green algae, elder berries, hawthorn fruits, rose hips, horsetail, shepherd's purse.

Carotenes: Found in carrots, cabbage, winter squash, sweet potatoes, dark leafy greens, apricots, spirulina, seaweeds. Herbal sources: peppermint, yellow dock, uva ursi, parsley, alfalfa, raspberry leaves, nettles, dandelion greens, kelp, green onions, violet leaves, cayenne, paprika, lamb's quarters, sage peppermint, chickweed, horsetail, black cohosh, rose hips.

Essential fatty acids (EFAs), including GLA, omega-6, and omega-3: Found in safflower oil, wheat germ oil. Herbal sources: all wild plants contain EFAs. Commercial sources: flax seed oil, evening primrose, black current, borage.

Boron: Found in organic fruits, vegetables, nuts. Herbal sources: all organic weeds, including chickweed, purslane, nettles, dandelion, yellow dock.

Calcium: Found in milk and dairy products, leafy greens, broccoli, clams, oysters, almonds, walnuts, sunflower seeds, sesame seeds (for example, tahini), legumes, tofu, softened bones of canned fish (sardines, mackerel, salmon), seaweed vegetables, whole grain, whey, shellfish. Herbal sources: valerian, kelp, nettles, horsetail, peppermint, sage, uva ursi, yellow dock chickweed, red clover, oatstraw, parsley, blackcurrant leaf, raspberry leaf, plantain leaf/seed, borage, dandelion leaf, amaranth leaves, lamb's quarter. Depleted by: coffee, sugar, salt, alcohol, cortisone enemas, too much phosphorus.

Chromium: Found in barley grass, bee pollen, prunes, nuts, mushrooms, liver, beets, whole wheat. Herbal sources: oatstraw, nettles, red clover, catnip, dulse, wild yam, yarrow, horsetail, black cohosh, licorice, echinacea, valerian, sarsaparilla. Depleted by: white sugar.

Copper: Found in liver, shellfish, nuts, legumes, water, organically grown grains, leafy greens, seaweeds, bittersweet chocolate. Herbal sources: skullcap, sage, horsetail, chickweed.

Iron: (Heme iron is easily absorbed by the body; non-heme iron not as easily absorbed, so should be taken with vitamin C.) Heme iron is found in liver, meat, poultry; non-heme iron is found in dried fruit, seeds, almonds, cashews, enriched and whole grains, legumes, green leafy vegetables. Herbal sources: chickweed, kelp, burdock, catnip, horsetail, Althea root, milk thistle seed, uva ursi, dandelion leaf/ root, yellow dock root, Dang Gui, black cohosh, echinacea, plantain leaves, sarsaparilla, nettles, peppermint, licorice, valerian, fenugreek. Depleted by: coffee, black tea, enemas, alcohol, aspirin, carbonated drinks, lack of protein, too much dairy.

Magnesium: Found in leafy greens, seaweeds, nuts, whole grains, yogurt, cheese, potatoes, corn, peas, squash. Herbal sources: oatstraw, licorice, kelp, nettle, dulse, burdock, chickweed, Althea root, horsetail, sage, raspberry leaf, red clover, valerian yellow dock, dandelion, carrot tops, parsley, evening primrose. Depleted by: hot flashes, night sweats, crying jags, alcohol, chemical diuretics, enemas, antibiotics, excessive fat intake.

Manganese: Found in any leaf or seed from a plant grown in healthy soil; seaweeds. Herbal sources: raspberry leaf, uva ursi, chickweed, milk thistle, yellow dock, ginseng, wild yam, hops, catnip, echinacea, horsetail, kelp, nettles, dandelion.

Molybdenum: Found in organically raised dairy products, legumes, grains, leafy greens. Herbal sources: nettles, dandelion greens, sage, oatstraw, fenugreek, raspberry leaves, red clover, horsetail, chickweed, seaweeds.

Nickel: Found in chocolate, nuts, dried beans, cereals. Herbal sources: alfalfa, red clover, oatstraw, fenugreek.

Phosphorus: Found in whole grains, seeds, nuts. Herbal sources: peppermint, yellow dock, milk thistle, fennel, hops, chickweed, nettles, dandelion, parsley, dulse, red clover. Depleted by: antacids.

Potassium: Found in celery, cabbage, peas, parsley, broccoli, peppers, carrots, potato skins, eggplant, whole grains, pears, citrus, seaweeds. Herbal sources: sage, catnip, hops, dulse, peppermint, skullcap, kelp, red clover, horsetail, nettles, borage, plantain. Depleted by: frequent hot flashes with sweating, night sweats, coffee, sugar, salt, alcohol, enemas, vomiting, diarrhea, chemical diuretics, dieting.

Selenium: Found in dairy products, seaweeds, grains, garlic, liver, kidneys, fish, shellfish. Herbal sources: catnip, milk thistle, valerian, dulse, black cohosh, ginseng, uva ursi, hops, echinacea, kelp, raspberry leaf, rose buds and hips, hawthorn berries, fenugreek, sarsaparilla, yellow dock.

Silicon: Found in unrefined grains, root vegetables, spinach, leeks. Herbal sources: horsetail, dulse, echinacea, cornsilk, burdock, oatstraw, licorice, chickweed, uva ursi, sarsaparilla.

Sulfur: Found in eggs, dairy products, cabbage family plants, onions, garlic, parsley, watercress. Herbal sources: nettles, sage, plantain horsetail.

Zinc: Found in oysters, seafood meat, liver, eggs, whole grains, wheat germ, pumpkin seeds, spirulina. Herbal sources: skullcap, sage, wild yam, chickweed, echinacea, nettles, dulse, milk thistle, sarsaparilla. Depleted by: alcohol, air pollution.

Herbs and Moves for Below the Belt

This is essential information for all women approaching 50 and beyond. Pass it on!

For Vaginal Dryness and Irritation (or Vaginitis)

First, avoid the following, as they aggravate vaginal dryness:

- ➤ Coffee.
- ➤ Alcohol.
- ➤ White sugar.
- ➤ Severe stress.
- ➤ Steroid/cortisone drugs. (Note: Vaginal anti-itch creams contain cortisol and should be used as a last resort; cortisone contributes to osteoporosis.)

Natural "Household" Vaginal Lubricants

- ➤ Coconut oil.
- ➤ Raw egg white.
- ➤ Honey.

- Aloe vera gel (bottled or fresh).
- Olive oil.
- Vegetable oil.
- Vitamin E oil.
- Ingest each day some omega-3 fatty acids, such as flax seed oils.
- Vitamin B12 supplements.

Other Natural/Herbal Remedies

- Comfrey root sitz bath. Brew two quarts/liters of the infusion, rewarm, strain, and soak in a "sitz" for five to 10 minutes several times a week.
- Drink only water for your beverages.
- Drink a special "rice broth," which works as an internal moisturizer: Boil a small handful of rice in 16 oz/500 ml or more of water to make a thin broth.
- Before making love, chew on a piece of Dang Gui root to increase vaginal lubrication.
- Use chickweed tincture, 25–40 drops in water, several times a day for two to four weeks.
- 25 drops motherwort tincture or 1–3 teaspoons of safflower or flaxseed oil can help to increase vaginal lubrication and thicken vaginal walls.
- Acidophilus capsules inserted vaginally help prevent yeast infections and create copious amounts of lubrication. Insert one or two capsules two to four hours before love-making.
- Comfrey ointment. Rub in morning and night and use as a lubricant. The vulva will be noticeably plumper and moister within three weeks.

➤ Use slippery elm as a soothing vaginal gel. Slowly heat 2 tablespoons slippery elm bark in a cup of water, stirring until thick. Cool before spreading over and inside the vulva and vagina. The gel lubricates, heals, and nourishes.

➤ Ointment made from wild yam roots acts as an "estrogen cream" and restore moistness and elasticity.

➤ Mix essential oil of *Salvia sclarea* with olive oil and apply to dry vaginal tissues that have lost their elasticity.

More Conventional Supplements

➤ Polycarbophil, the active ingredient in many over-the-counter vaginal creams, pulls water into vaginal cells, helping restore and maintain healthy lubrication. It also reduces vaginal infections by making the vagina more alkaline.

➤ Estrogens creams are available everywhere. The only problem is that, even when applied vaginally, they are absorbed by the blood and will carry many of the same risks as taking oral estrogens. So if you do not want estrogen side effects, this may not be the best route. You can also purchase estrogen and testosterone creams.

➤ Progesterone cream lubricates the vagina, but doesn't have the side effects of estrogen creams. These creams naturally derived from wild yam roots.

To relieve SEVERE vaginal itching and burning:

➣ Belladonna.

➣ Cantharis.

➣ Sulfur.

➣ Natrum mur.

➣ Motherwort tincture: 10 to 20 drops several times a day.

➣ Plantian oil or ointment.

> Brew a quart/liter of nettle infusion several times a week. Either sit in it through a sitz bath, or drink it.

> Calendula cream applied morning.

> Take an oat or honey bath. (You can put honey on a pad and wear it, as it draws in moisture.)

> A comfrey root or chamomile blossom compress. Infuse the comfrey and soak a towel in it, or make some chamomile tea and use the teabag. Apply either.

Vaginal Exercises

1. Try to bring yourself to an orgasm alone or with a partner.

2. Pelvic Floor Exercises:

   > Breathe out and push down as though you were trying to push something out of your vagina. Hold for three seconds, then inhale and relax. Do 25–50 reps.

   > To tone vaginal muscles and increase lubrication: Tighten the inner muscles of the vagina around a finger or small, smooth marble and hold for 10 to 13 seconds; pulse (contract and relax) your vaginal muscles rapidly (10–30 times) as you breathe out. Repeat 10-25 times.

   > To tone vagina and bladder: Sit in a bathtub with water up to your hips. See if you can suck water into your vagina and expel it. Suck in as you breathe in; push out as you breathe out. Do 25–50 times.

To Improve Bladder Control or Incontinence

Note: Roughly 75 percent of women will experience one or more incidents of urinary incontinence after menopause. This may result in "stress incontinence" (leakage when laughing, sneezing, coughing, or picking something up, running, and other normal activities that put stress on the bladder). It may also be experienced as "urge incontinence" (leakage as soon as the urge comes on, except there is no time to get to the toilet). Damaged or weakened pelvic floor muscles are the cause, which many women damage during childbirth. Other aggravating factors include alcohol use, urinary tract infections, fibroids, and chronic constipation.

Avoid the following bladder irritants:

> ➤ Caffeine.

> ➤ Alcohol.

> ➤ White sugar.

> ➤ Citrus.

> ➤ Tomatoes.

> ➤ Cayenne.

> ➤ Hot peppers.

> ➤ Iced drinks.

> ➤ Carbonated drinks.

> ➤ Pineapple.

> ➤ Smoking increases your risk of developing stress incontinence by 350 percent!

> ➤ Many common drugs trigger incontinence: diuretics, antidepressants, beta-blockers, blood pressure–lowering drugs, sleeping pills, tranquilizers.

Herbal Remedies

➤ Pulsatilla.

➤ Zincum.

➤ Boil dried teasel *(Dipsacus sylvestris)* roots with a tablespoon to a cup of water for 10 to 15 minutes, and then drink daily.

➤ Replace your coffee with cranberry juice.

➤ Antispasmodic herbs such as black cohosh, ginger, catnip, and cornsilk may urge incontinence.

➤ Yarrow *(Achillea milefolium)* will help heal bladder infections, incontinence, and heavy periods, but may aggravate hot flashes. Recommended as a tea or infusion of the dried flowers as desired, or as a tincture of the fresh flowering tops, 5–10 drops, two to three times daily.

Conventional Remedies

➤ ERT/HRT and estrogen vaginal creams are highly effective at reversing incontinence caused by vaginal and bladder wall thinning.

Bladder Control Exercises

1. Pelvic floor exercises (see page 196).

2. While-you-pee exercises:

   ➢ Kegel exercises isolate the tiny muscles that start and stop your urinary stream. (In other words, next time you pee, stop the flow.) Hold as long as you can (work up to at least 10 seconds) before letting go and peeing again. Practice this every time you urinate. (You can also do this when you're not urinating to strengthen the muscle.)

➤ Pulse your urine flow by pushing out very strongly, then slackening it off until it's just a dribble, then push out again, and so on. Repeat as many times as possible every time you urinate.

➤ Empty the bladder completely every time you void by pressing down behind your pubic bone with fingertips or the flat of your palm.

➤ Scheduled toileting. Go on a regular schedule, say, every 60–90 minutes. After three to four consecutive dry days, increase the interval by 15–30 minutes, and keep increasing until you're at every 4 hours.

3. Other exercises:

➤ Push hard on the very top of the head to relieve urge incontinence on the spot.

➤ Set out two shallow basins: one with very hot water, the other with cold. Start by relaxing for three minutes in the hot one. Then lower yourself up and down, in and out of the icy water for one minute. Repeat three to four times; do it several times a week.

Where to Go for More Information

For more information about disease prevention and wellness, visit me online at *www.sarahealth.com*, where you will find more than 300 links—including these—related to your good health and wellness.

General Gynecological Health

American Health Care Association: *www.ahca.org*

American Medical Women's Association (AMWA): *www.amwa-doc.org*

National Women's Health Resource Center: *www.healthywomen.org*

Health Oasis: Mayo Clinic: *www.mayohealth.org/mayo/ common/htm/index.htm*

Women's Health Information Center: *www.ourbodiesourselves.org*

Healthy Way Sympatico Health (comprehensive health site for Canadians, with extensive list of reviewed links). *www.gt.sympatico.ca/Contents/Health/health.html*

GYN 101 (information on how to be an informed healthcare consumer, especially for younger women): *www.gyn101.com*

Salon.com (harp, engaging web magazine for women with lots of great health information and advice): *www.salon.com*

General Health

American Health Care Association: *www.ahca.org*

The Canadian Medical Association: *www.cma.ca*

American Medical Association: *www.ama-assn.org*

Pharmaceutical Information Network (Pharm InfoNet) (good resource for drug development information): *www.pharminfo.com*

American Medical Association Medical Glossary (help with terms that may be used in an informed consent document): *www.ama-assn.org/insight.genhlth/glossary/index.htm*

Food and Drug Administration (FDA) (regulations and information on drugs and other products): *www.fda.gov*

National Institute of Health (NIH) (dedicated to providing the public with the latest information about different health issues and ongoing scientific research/special reports): *www.nih.gov*

Center for Medical Consumers and Health Care Information: *www.medicalconsumers.org*

Intelihealth (home to Johns Hopkins health information, as well as the U.S. Pharmacopeia database): *www.intelihealth.com*

Mediconsult.com (A–Z medical directory with drug information, fitness and nutrition, news briefs, online events and forums and chat) : *www.mediconsult.com*

Health Information Highway (comprehensive health care resource with discussion groups): *www.stayhealthy.com*

Merck Manual (one of the most popular manuals used by doctors worldwide. Detailed information about thousands of conditions): *www.merck.com*

Healthy Way at Sympatico.ca (good source of information organized by medical condition. Self-assessment resources, useful links and monthly magazine): *www.healthyway.sympatico.ca*

Family Internet (information on diseases, conditions, treatments, prognoses, etc. With a health and diet file): *www.familyinternet.com*

Online Pharmacies

www.drugstore.com

www.soma.com

www.planetRx.com

www.genrx.com

www.pharmweb.net

www.cponline.gsm.com (Clinical Pharmacology Online)

Drug Databases

www.rxlist.com: free, searchable database of more than 4,000 prescription and over-the-counter medications

pharminfo/drugdb/dbmnv.htnl: drug data with links to articles

Natural/Alternative Medications and Therapies

MotherNature.com: information on what natural remedies do and how to take them

Homeopathy Online: *www.homeopathonline.com*

EarthMed.com: world's largest Website dedicated to natural and alternative, practitioners, products and services.

Finding a Doctor

Royal College of Physicians and Surgeons of Canada: *rcpsc.medica.org*

Menopause

The Menopause Center
P.O. Box 1339
Suquamish, WA 98392-1339
(360) 598–3688
e-mail: mtimes@telebyte.net

Note: This organization publishes the newsletter MenoTimes, published and edited by Brenda Beeley, a licensed acupuncturist, classical homeopath, and herbalist. She is a graduate of the Hahnemann College of Homeopathy and the San Francisco College of Acupuncture.

North American Menopause Society (NAMS)
P.O. Box 94527
Cleveland, OH 44101
(216) 844–8748
e-mail:info@menopause.org
www.menopause.org

General Websites Related to Women's Health

[Note: This is adapted from a thorough "best women's health on the web" review as of 2000 by the American Journal of Public Health. Volume 90(9), September, 2000, pp. 1475–1476.]

Centers for Disease Control and Prevention Women's Health
www.cdc.gov/health/womensmenu.htm

HRSA Women's Health Resources
www.hrsa.gov/WomensHealth/resources.htm
www.hrsa.gov/WomensHealth/wh_orgs.htm

HRSA Resources for Women
www.bphc.hrsa.dhhs.gov/cc/resourceswomen.htm

Global Health Network-Women's Health
www.pitt.edu/HOME/GHNet/GHWomen.html

National Institutes of Health Office of Research on
Women's Health (ORWH) links
www4.od.nih.gov/orwh/other.html

New York Times Women's Health Resource Links
www.nytimes.com/specials/women/whome/resources.html

Society for Women's Health Research Women's Health
Facts and Links
www.womens-health.org/factsheet.html

United Nations Gender and AIDS Links
unaidsapict.inet.co.th/gend.htm

University of Chicago Health Education Catalog
uhs.bsd.uchicago.edu/uhs/health.ed.catalog.html

US Food and Drug Administration Non-government
Sources of Women's Health Information
vm.cfsan.fda.gov/~ dms/wh-ngov.html

Web Sites for Women's Health *http://umbc7.umbc.edu/*
~ korenman/wmst/links_hlth.html

WHO links Family and Reproductive Health
http://www.who.org/home/map_ht.html#Family and
Reproductive Health

Women's Health Interactive Resource Center
www.womens-health.com/resources/index.html

WWWomen Search Directory: Health
www.wwwomen.com/category/health1.html

Individual Websites

Agency for Healthcare Research and Quality Women's Health *www.ahcpr.gov/research/womenix.htm*

American Medical Women's Association *www.amwa-doc.org/*

Amnesty International Female Genital Mutilation Information *www.amnesty.org/ailib/intcam/femgen/fgm1.htm*

Canadian Women's Health Network *www.cwhn.ca/*

Center for Reproductive Law and Policy *www.crlp.org/*

Center for Women Policy Studies *www.centerwomenpolicy.org/*

Commonwealth Fund Commission on Women's Health *www.cmwf.org/programs/women/index.asp*

Department of Health and Human Services National Centers of Excellence in Women's Health *www.4woman.gov/owh/coe/index.htm*

Female Genital Mutilation Education and Networking Project *www.fgmnetwork.org/*

Forum for Women's Health *www.womenshealth.org/*

Girl Power Campaign US Department of Health and Human Services *http://www.health.org/gpower/index.htm*

Alan Guttmacher Institute *http://www.agi-usa.org/*

Harvard Law School Database on Law and Population *www.law.harvard.edu/programs/annual_review/*

Harvard University Global Reproductive Health Forum *www.hsph.harvard.edu/Organizations/healthnet/*

Health Resources and Services Administration Women's Health Information *www.hrsa.gov/WomensHealth/*

Health Resources and Services Administration Bureau of Primary Health Care Office of Minority and Women's Health
www.bphc.hrsa.dhhs.gov/cc/healthywomen.htm

JAMA Women's Health Information Center
www.ama-assn.org/special/womh/womh.htm

Mayo Clinic Women's Health Center *http://www.mayo.ivi.com/mayo/common/htm/womenpg.htm*

Medscape: Women's Health
WomensHealth.medscape.com/Home/Topics/WomensHealth/womenshealth.html

National Center for Health Statistics, Centers for Disease Control and Prevention. *www.cdc.gov/nchswww/*

National Council on Women's Health *www.ncwh.org/*

National Institute of Mental Health Office for Special Populations *www.nimh.nih.gov/osp/*

National Institute on Drug Abuse Women and Gender Research
www.nida.nih.gov/WHGD/WHGDHome.html

National Institutes of Health Office of Research on Women's Health *www4.od.nih.gov/orwh/*

National Institutes of Health National Heart, Lung, and Blood Institute Women's Health Initiative
www.nhlbi.nih.gov/whi/index.html

National Council on Women's Health
www.womens-health.com/affiliations/affiliates/ncwh/index.html

National Women's Health Information Center
www.4woman.org/nwhic/

New York Times Women's Health
www.nytimes.com/specials/women/whome/index.html

North American Menopause Society
www.menopause.org/

OBGYN Net Resources for Women
www.obgyn.net/women/women.asp

Planned Parenthood *www.plannedparenthood.org/*

Public Health Service Coordinating Committee on Women's
Health *www.hrsa.gov/WomensHealth/phs_cc.htm*

Society for Women's Health Research
www.womens-health.org/

University of Illinois at Chicago Center for Research on
Women and Gender
www.uic.edu/depts/crwg/outline.htm

University of Maryland Women's Health Links
www.MarylandWomensHealth.org/whrg/riderx.html

University of Wisconsin Women's Health Web
www.medsch.wisc.edu/chslib/hw/womens/

US Food and Drug Administration (FDA) Office of
Women's Health *www.fda.gov/womens/default.htm*

Women's Health Interactive *www.womens-health.com/*

World Health Organization *http://www.who.org/*

Bibliography

Beard, M.D., F.A.C.O.G., Mary K., and Lindsay R. Curtis, M.D., FACOG. *Menopause and the Years Ahead,* (Fisher Books: 1988. Tuscon, Ariz.).

Benedict S. et al. "Breast cancer detection by daughters of women with breast cancer." *Cancer Practice*, 1997 Jul, Vol 5:213 –219.

Bequaert Holmes, Helen. "A Call to Heal Medicine" in *Feminist Perspectives in Medical Ethics*. Edited by Helen Bequaert Holmes and Laura M. Purdy. (Indiana University Press, 1992).

Bernstein, Leslie and Kelsey, Jennifer L. "Epidemiology and Prevention of Breast Cancer." Department of Health Research and Policy, Stanford University, and Department of Preventive Medicine, University of Southern California (1996): 47–67.

"Body of evidence: the effects of cholrine on human health." Booklet. Greenpeace, 1994.

Bondy, M. and Mastromarino, C. "Ethical issues of genetic testing and their implications in epidemiologic studies *Annals of Epidemiology*. July 1997, Volume 7: 363–366.

Bove, C.M. et al. "Presymptomatic and predisposition genetic testing: ethical and social considerations. *Semin Oncol Nurs* 1997 May 13:135-140.

Brody, J, et al. *Mapping the history of pesticide use in the Cape Cod Breast Cancer and Environment Study.* Paper presented at the World Conference on Breast Cancer, July 13–17, 1997, Kingston, Ontario, Canada.

"Calcium supplements not equally effective." Reuters, Dec 27, 1999. (SOURCE: *American Journal of Therapeutics* 1999; 6:303–311, 313–321 and *Journal of Clinical Pharmacology* 1999;39:1-4).

"Calories Count In Colon Cancer Risk." *American Journal of Epidemiology*, 1997;145:199-210.

Canadian Hypertension Society. "High Blood Pressure and Drug Treatment." 1999.

"Cancer center studies link between dietary fat and breast cancer. *Cancer Researcher Weekly,* 28 February 1994: 8. Report on a University of California, Irvine, CA, study.

"Cancer In Massachusetts Town Cause By Demographics, Not Environment." *The Boston Globe*, Jan 15, 1997.

Caplan, L.S. Disparities in breast cancer screening: is it ethical? *Public Health Review* 1997, Vol 25: 31-41.

Casper, Robert F., and Alcide Chapdelaine, "Estrogen and Interrupted Progestin: a New Concept for Menopausal Hormone Replacement Therapy." *Ameican Journal of Obstetrics and Gynecology*, Volume 168, April 1993.

Casstevens, Rebecca. *Addressing current uses of pesticides linked with breast cancer.* Paper presented at the World Conference on Breast Cancer, July13–17, 1997, Kingston, Ontario, Canada.

Chang, Trina. "Simplifying Breast Cancer Diagnosis." *American Health,* April 1997, 18.

Cicala, Roger S., M.D. *The Heart Disease Sourcebook,* Lowell House, 1998.

Clute, Eva, MPH. *Tamoxifen—Breast cancer preventive or human carcinogen: 1997 update.* Paper presented at the World Conference on Breast Cancer, July13–17, 1997, Kingston, Ontario, Canada.

Colborn, Theo, John Peterson Myers, Dianne Dumanoski, *Our Stolen Future.* (Dutton, New York, 1996.)

Coney, Sandra. *The Menopause Industry: How the Medical Establishment Exploits Women.* (Hunter House, Calif.)

Delanet, Kathy, R.N., B.S.N. and Marie R. Squillace, M.A., *Living with Heart Disease.* Lowell House, 1998.

DeMarco, Carolyn. "Preserving our environment: Breast cancer and the environment." *Health Naturally,* issue no. 18 (October/November 1995): 26–30.

DeMarco, Carolyn. "The great mammogram debate: Are we spending millions to do naught for ought?" *Wellness MD,* vol. 3, no. 1 (January/February 1993).

Dickens, Bernard M., Nancy Pei, and Kathryn M. Taylor, "Legal and Ethical Issues in Genetic Testing and Counselling for Susceptibility to Breast, Ovarian and Colon Cancer." *Canadian Medical Association Journal,* March 15, 1996; 154 (6):813–818.

Doan, Brian D. et al. *Psychological issues facing high risk women seeking genetic testing for hereditary breast cancer.* Paper presented at the World Conference on Breast Cancer, July 13–17, 1997, Kingston, Ontario, Canada.

Doress, Paula Brown, Diana Laskin Seigal, and the Midlife and Older Women Book Project in Cooperation with the Boston Women's Health Collective. *Ourselves Growing Older:* (New York: Simon and Schuster,1987).

Eight Biennial Report On Great Lakes Water Quality, Under the Great Lakes Water Quality Agreement of 1978 to the Governments of the United States and Canda and the State and Provincial Governments of the Great Lakes Basin. International Joint Commission, 1250 23rd Street NW, Suite 100, Washington , D.C. 20440. 1996.

Emanuel, Ezekiel J. and Linda L. Emanuel, "Four models of the physician-patient relationship." *Journal of the American Medical Association,* 1992, 267 (16): 2221–2226.

Epstein, Samuel S., M.D., and David Steinmean with Suzanne LeVert, *The Breast Cancer Prevention Program: The First Complete Survey of the Causes of Breast Cancer and the Steps You Can Take to Reduce Your Risks.* (New York: Macmillan, 1998).

Etchells, E et al. "Disclosure." *CMAJ.* 1996, 155:387–91.

———. "Voluntariness." *CMAJ.* 1996, 155:1083–6.

Etchells, E, Gilbert Sharpe et al. "Consent." *Canadian Medical Association Journal.* 1996, 155:177-80.

Everyday Carcinogens: Stopping Cancer Before It Starts. Proceedings from the March 1999 workshop on primary cancer prevention, McMaster University, Hamilton, Ontario, Canada.

Evista patient information. Eli Lilly and Company, Indianapolis, IN 46285, USA PA 2091, printed 1999.

Findlay, Deborah and Leslia Miller. "Medical power and women's bodies." In B.S. Bolaria and R. Bolaria, eds. *Women, Medicine and Health* (Halifax: Fernwood 1994).

Fletcher, S.W. Whither scientific deliberation in health policy recommendations? Alice in the wonderland of breast-cancer screening. *N Engl J Med* 1997; 336:1180–3.

Fletcher, Suzanne W., Confusion about Breast-Cancer Screening. *N Engl J Med* 1997; 336:1465–71.

Fugh-Berman, Adriane. *Alternative Medicine: What Works* (Tucson, Ariz.: Odonian Press 1996)

Gofman, John W., M.D., Ph.D. *Preventing Breast Cancer: The Story of a Major, Proven, Preventable Cause of This Disease.* (San Francisco, Calif.: CNR Book Division, Committee for Nuclear Responsibility, 1995)

Greenwood, Sadja, M.D., *Menopause Naturally: Preparing for the Second Half of Life* (Calif.: Volcano Press 1992.)

Gunawant, Deepika M.D. and Warrier, Gopi. *Ayurveda: The Ancient Indian Healing Tradition.* Element: 1997.

Healy, Bernadette, M.D. "BRCA Genes — Bookmaking, Fortunetelling, and Medical Care." *The New England Journal of Medicine,* 336(20): 1448–1449: May 15, 1997.

"IFIC Review: Uses and Nutritional Impact of Fat Reduction Ingredients, International Food Information Council 1100 Connecticut Avenue N.W., Suite 430, Washington D.C. 20036, October 1995.

Kra, J., Siegfried, M.D., FACP. *What Every Woman Must Know About Heart Disease.* (New York City: Warner Books, 1996).

Kushi, Mishio. *The Cancer Prevention Guide.* New York: St. Martin's Press, 1993.

Lad, Dr. Vasant. *Ayurveda: the Science of Self-Healing.* Lotus Press: 1984.

Lark, Susan M., M.D. *The Menopause Self Help Book.* Celestial Arts, 1990.

Lee, John R., M.D., *What Your Doctor May Not Tell You About Menopause* (New York: 1996, Warner Books)

Levine, R.J. *Ethics and Regulation of Clinical Research.* (New Haven, Conn.:Yale University Press,1988.)

Love, Susan M.D., and Karen Lindsey, *Dr. Susan Love's Breast Book, 2nd Edition*. New York: Addison-Wesley, 1995.

Mastroianni, Anna C., Ruth Faden, and Daniel Federman, Editors. *Women and Health Research: Ethical and Legal Issues of Including Women in Clinical Studies*, Volume 1. (Washington National Academy Press, 1994.)

McAuliffe, Kathleen, "Dying Of Embarrassment." *More*, May/June, 1999:52–62.

Morrison, Judith H. *The Book of Ayurveda*. New York: Simon and Schuster: 1995.

National Institutes of Health Consensus Statement. Breast cancer screening for women ages 40–49, January 21–23, 1997. Bethesda, Md.: National Cancer Institute, 1997.

Nechas, Eileen and Denise Foley. *Unequal Treatment: What You Don't Know About How Women Are Mistreated by the Medical Community* (New York: Simon and Schuster,1994.)

Osteoporosis Society of Canada, "Biophosphates." Fact Sheet Series Number 9, 1999.

———. "Cacitonin: Its Role in the Treatment of Osteoporosis," Press Release, November, 1999.

———. "Calcium." Fact Sheet Series Number 3, 1999.

———. "Hormone Therapy" Fact Sheet Series Number 8, 1999.

———. "Living With Osteoporosis." Fact Sheet Series Number 1, 1999.

———. "SERMS: Their role in the Prevention of Osteoporosis," Press Release, December 1998.

Perry, Susan and Katherine O'Hanlan, M.D. *Natural Menopause: The Complete Guide to a Woman's Most Misunderstood Passage,* (New York: Addison-Wesley Publishing, 1992.)

Rosenthal, M. Sara. *Women of the Sixties Turning 50* (2000, Penguin Canada, Toronto.)

———. *Managing PMS Naturally* (Toronto: Penguin Canada, 2001.)

———. *The Gynecological Sourcebook, 4th Edition* (New York: McGraw-Hill, 2003.)

———. *50 Ways Women Can Prevent Heart Disease* (New York: McGraw-Hill, 2000.)

———. *The Breast Sourcebook*, 2nd Edition (New York: McGraw-Hill,1999.).

————. *50 Ways To Prevent Colon Cancer* (New York: McGraw-Hill, 1999.)

————. *The Gastrointestinal Sourcebook* (New York: McGraw-Hill, 1997.)

————. *Stopping Cancer At The Source* (Toronto: SarahealthPress, 2001.)

————. *Women Managing Stress* (Toronto: Penguin Books, 2002.)

Rosser, Sue V. *Women's Health—Missing from U.S. Medicine* (Indiana: Indiana University Press, 1994.)

Rudd, Dr. Wm. Warren, *Advice From The Rudd Clinic: A Guide To Colorectal Health* (Toronto: Macmillan Canada, 1997.)

Sherwin, Susan, "Feminist and Medical Ethics: Two Different Approaches to Contextual Ethics" in *Feminist Perspectives in Medical Ethics*. Edited by Helen Bequaert Holmes and Laura M. Purdy (Indiana: Indiana University Press, 1992.)

Sherwin, Susan, *Patient No Longer: Feminist Ethics and Health Care*. (Philidelphia: Temple University Press, 1984.)

Shimer, Porter, *Keeping Fitness Simple: 500 Tips for Fitting Exercise into Your Life*. (Pownal Vt.: Storey Books, 1998.)

Soto, Ana M., Kerrie L. Chung, and Carlos Sonnenschein, "The Pesticides Endosulfan, Toxaphene, and Dieldrin Have Estrogenic Effets on Human Estrogen-Sensitive Cells." *Environmental Health Perspectives*, vol 102, February, 1994.

Steingraber, Sandra, *Living Downstream: An Ecologist Looks At Cancer and the Environment*. (New York : Addison-Wesley,1997.)

Warren, Virgina, L. "Feminist Directions in Medical Ethics" *Feminist Perspectives in Medical Ethics*, Edited by Helen Bequaert Holmes and Laura M. Purdy (Indiana: Indiana University Press, 1992).

Weed, Susun S., *Wise Woman Ways: Menopausal Years*. (Woodstock, N.Y.: Ash Tree Publishing, 1992.)

Weed, Susun S. *Menopausal Years: The Wise Woman Way— Alternative Approaches for Women 30-90*. (Woodstock, N.Y.: Ash Tree Publishing, 1992.)

Zimmerman, Mary K, "The Women's Health Movement: A Critique of Medical Enterprise and the Position of Women" in M. Farle & B. Hess (Eds.), *Analysing Gender*. (Sage, 1987).

Index

A

abdominal cramps,130, 134, 135
a-BHC, 93
abortion, 97-98
absorption, maximizing calcium, 165
acupuncture, 54, 161
aerobic exercise, 80, 83
alcohol consumption, 60, 61
alcohol, 75-76, 86, 87
alpha-blocking agents, 62
androgen, natural, 171
anemia, 39, 135, 138
animal products, 117
anoscope exam, 139
anticonvulsants, 151
antidepressant, 53, 60
appetite suppressants, 60
arterial plaque, 51, 58, 59
ascorbic acid, 40
Ayurvedic medicine, 147

B

back pain, 64-65
bacterial breast infection, 90
bad cholesterol, 55-58, 70, 74, 80, 142, 162
bad habits, breast cancer and, 86-87
barium enema, 140-141
baseline mammograms, 32
beta-blockers, 58, 62
bilateral mastectomy, 104

bilateral oophorectomy, 28-29
bioflavonoids, 40, 117
biphosphonates, 163-164
birth control pills, 34, 60, 95
bladder cancer, 51
bladder control exercises, 198-199
bladder irritants, 197
bladder problems, stress-induced, 64
bleeding,34-35, 37, 121, 135
blood calcium level, 151
blood clot, 11, 12, 112
blood glucose, 72
blood pressure, 51-79
blood sugar, 62, 66, 72
blood tests, 32, 139-140
blood-thinning herbs, 78
bone densitometry, 161
bone health, 149-170
bone loss, 152-164
bone mass, exercise and, 168-170
bone,
    cortical, 151
    trabecular, 151
bone-building drugs, 36
bowel diseases, 128-136
bowel movements, 74, 123-124, 138
bowel,
    lazy, 124-125
    retraining your, 127-128
BRCA 1, 2, and 3 gene, 102-103
breast bleeding, 121
breast cancer, 86-114

About the Author

Dr. M. Sara Rosenthal is a bioethicist and sociologist with a long career as medical health journalist. She is author of more than 25 widely-recommended health books, including *The Gynecological Sourcebook, 4th Edition* (McGraw-Hill, 2003) which is recommended by *Ladies' Home Journal*. Her work covers everything from women's reproductive health issues to general health, and has been translated into languages as diverse as Chinese, Arabic, Polish, Russian, and Spanish. Her work is reviewed and reprinted on over 500 Websites, and she is a frequent contributor to *WebMD.com*. Dr. Rosenthal received both masters and Ph.D. in sociology and bioethics from the university of Toronto's Joint Centre for Bioethics, the only World Health Organization collaborating center in bioethics. Dr. Rosenthal is now Assistant Professor, Bioethics, Department of Behavioral Science and the University of Kentucky College of Medicine.

Other books by M. Sara Rosenthal

The Thyroid Sourcebook (4th edition, 2000)

The Gynecological Sourcebook (4th edition, 2003)

[Canadian edition of above: Gynecological Health]

The Pregnancy Sourcebook (3rd edition, 1999)

The Fertility Sourcebook (3rd edition, 2002)

The Breastfeeding Sourcebook (2nd edition 1998)

The Breast Sourcebook (2nd edition, 1999)

The Gastrointestinal Sourcebook (1997;1998)

The Type 2 Diabetic Woman (1999)

The Thyroid Sourcebook for Women (1999)

Women and Depression (2000)

Women of the '60s Turning 50 (Canada Only 2000)

Women and Passion (Canada Only 2000)

Managing PMS Naturally (2001)

Women Managing Stress (2002)

The Canadian Type 2 Diabetes Sourcebook (Canada only; 2002)

The Hypothyroid Sourcebook (2002)

The Natural Woman's Guide To Preventing Diabetes Complications (2002)

The Natural Woman's Guide To Hormone Replacement Therapy (2003)

50 Ways Series

50 Ways To Prevent Colon Cancer (2000)

50 Ways Women Can Prevent Heart Disease (2000)

50 Ways To Manage Ulcer, Heartburn and Reflux (2001)

50 Ways To Manage Type 2 Diabetes (U.S. only; 2001)

50 Ways To Prevent and Manage Stress (2001)

50 Ways To Prevent Depression Without Drugs (2001)

SarahealthGuides™

These are M. Sara Rosenthal's own line of health books written by herself and other health authors. SarahealthGuides are dedicated to rare, controversial or stigmatizing health topics you won't find in regular bookstores. SarahealthGuides are available at only online bookstores such as amazon.com. Visit *www.sarahealth.com* for upcoming titles.

Stopping Cancer At The Source (2001)

Women and Unwanted Hair (2001)

Living Well With Celiac Disease by Claudine Crangle (2002)

The Thyroid Cancer Book (2002)

Living Well With Ostomy (2003) by Elizabeth Rayson

Thyroid Eye Disease (2003) by Elaine Moore